Pacchiarotto with Other Poems by Robert Browning

Robert Browning is one of the most significant Victorian Poets and, of course, English Poetry.

Much of his reputation is based upon his mastery of the dramatic monologue although his talents encompassed verse plays and even a well-regarded essay on Shelley during a long and prolific career.

He was born on May 7th, 1812 in Walmouth, London. Much of his education was home based and Browning was an eclectic and studious student, learning several languages and much else across a myriad of subjects, interests and passions.

Browning's early career began promisingly. The fragment from his intended long poem Pauline brought him to the attention of Dante Gabriel Rossetti, and was followed by Paracelsus, which was praised by both William Wordsworth and Charles Dickens. In 1840 the difficult Sordello, which was seen as willfully obscure, brought his career almost to a standstill.

Despite these artistic and professional difficulties his personal life was about to become immensely fulfilling. He began a relationship with, and then married, the older and better known Elizabeth Barrett. This new foundation served to energise his writings, his life and his career.

During their time in Italy they both wrote much of their best work. With her untimely death in 1861 he returned to London and thereafter began several further major projects.

The collection Dramatis Personae (1864) and the book-length epic poem The Ring and the Book (1868-69) were published and well received; his reputation as a venerated English poet now assured.

Robert Browning died in Venice on December 12th, 1889.

Index of Contents

PACCHIAROTTO AND HOW HE WORKED IN DISTEMPER WITH OTHER POEMS

PROLOGUE

Oh, the old wall here! How I could pass
Life in a long midsummer day,
My feet confined to a plot of grass,
My eyes from a wall not once away!

And lush and lithe do the creepers clothe
Yon wall I watch, with a wealth of green:
Its bald red bricks draped, nothing loth,
In lappets of tangle they laugh between.

Now, what is it makes pulsate the robe?
Why tremble the sprays? What life o'erbrims
The body,—the house, no eye can probe,—
Divined as, beneath a robe, the limbs?

And there again! But my heart may guess
Who tripped behind; and she sang perhaps:
So, the old wall throbbed, and its life's excess
Died out and away in the leafy wraps!

Wall upon wall are between us: life
And song should away from heart to heart!
I—prison-bird, with a ruddy strife
At breast, and a lip whence storm-notes start—

Hold on, hope hard in the subtle thing
That 's spirit: though cloistered fast, soar free;
Account as wood, brick, stone, this ring
Of the rueful neighbors, and—forth to thee!

OF PACCHIAROTTO, AND HOW HE WORKED IN DISTEMPER

I

Query: was ever a quainter

Crotchet than this of the painter
Giacomo Pacchiarotto
Who took "Reform" for his motto?

II

He, pupil of old Fungaio,
Is always confounded (heigho!)
With Pacchia, contemporaneous
No question, but how extraneous
In the grace of soul, the power
Of hand,—undoubted dower
Of Pacchia who decked (as we know,
My Kirkup!) San Bernardino,
Turning the small dark Oratory
To Siena's Art-laboratory,
As he made its straitness roomy
And glorified its gloomy,
With Bazzi and Beccafumi.
(Another heigho for Bazzi:
How people miscall him Razzi!)

III

This Painter was of opinion
Our earth should be his dominion
Whose Art could correct to pattern
What Nature had slurred—the slattern!
And since, beneath the heavens,
Things lay now at sixes and sevens,
Or, as he said, sopra-sotto—
Thought the painter Pacchiarotto
Things wanted reforming, therefore.
"Wanted it"—ay, but wherefore?
When earth held one so ready
As he to step forth, stand steady
In the middle of God's creation
And prove to demonstration
What the dark is, what the light is,
What the wrong is, what the right is,
What the ugly, what the beautiful,
What the restive, what the dutiful,
In Mankind profuse around him?
Man, devil as now he found him,
Would presently soar up angel
At the summons of such evangel,

And owe—what would Man not owe
To the painter Pacchiarotto?
Ay, look to thy laurels, Giotto!

IV

But Man, he perceived, was stubborn,
Grew regular brute, once cub born;
And it struck him as expedient—
Ere he tried, to make obedient
The wolf, fox, bear, and monkey
By piping advice in one key,—
That his pipe should play a prelude
To something heaven-tinged not hell-hued,
Something not harsh but docile,
Man-liquid, not Man-fossil—
Not fact, in short, but fancy.
By a laudable necromancy
He would conjure up ghosts—a circle
Deprived of the means to work ill
Should his music prove distasteful
And pearls to the swine go wasteful.
To be rent of swine—that was hard!
With fancy he ran no hazard:
Pact might knock him o'er the mazard.

V

So, the painter Pacchiarotto
Constructed himself a grotto
In the quarter of Stalloreggi—
As authors of note allege ye.
And on each of the whitewashed sides of it
He painted—(none far and wide so fit
As he to perform in fresco)—
He painted nor cried quiesco
Till he peopled its every square foot
With Man—from the Beggar barefoot
To the Noble in cap and feather;
All sorts and conditions together.
The Soldier in breastplate and helmet
Stood frowningly—hail fellow well met—
By the Priest armed with bell, book, and candle.
Nor did he omit to handle
The Fair Sex, our brave distemperer:
Not merely King, Clown, Pope, Emperor—

He diversified too his Hades
Of all forms, pinched Labor and paid Ease,
With as mixed an assemblage of Ladies.

VI

Which work done, dry,—he rested him,
Cleaned palette, washed brush, divested him
Of the apron that suits frescanti,
And, bonnet on ear stuck jaunty,
This hand upon hip well planted,
That, free to wave as it wanted,
He addressed in a choice oration
His folk of each name and nation,
Taught its duty to every station.
The Pope was declared an arrant
Impostor at once, I warrant.
The Emperor—truth might tax him
With ignorance of the maxim
"Shear sheep but nowise flay them!"
And the Vulgar that obey them,
The Ruled, well-matched with the Ruling,
They failed not of wholesome schooling
On their knavery and their fooling.
As for Art—where 's decorum? Pooh-poohed it is
By Poets that plague us with lewd ditties,
And Painters that pester with nudities!

VII

Now, your rater and debater
Is balked by a mere spectator
Who simply stares and listens
Tongue-tied, while eye nor glistens
Nor brow grows hot and twitchy,
Nor mouth, for a combat itchy,
Quivers with some convincing
Reply—that sets him wincing?
Nay, rather—reply that furnishes
Your debater with just what burnishes
The crest of him, all one triumph,
As you see him rise, hear him cry "Humph!
Convinced am I? This confutes me?
Receive the rejoinder that suits me!
Confutation of vassal for prince meet—
Wherein all the powers that convince meet,

And mash my opponent to mincemeat!"

So, off from his head flies the bonnet,
His hip loses hand planted on it,
While t' other hand, frequent in gesture,
Slinks modestly back beneath vesture,
As—hop, skip and jump,—he 's along with
Those weak ones he late proved so strong with!
Pope, Emperor, lo, he 's beside them,
Friendly now, who late could not abide them,
King, Clown, Soldier, Priest, Noble, Burgess;
And his voice, that out-roared Boanerges,
How minikin-mildly it urges
In accents how gentled and gingered
Its word in defence of the injured!
"Oh, call him not culprit, this Pontiff!
Be hard on this Kaiser ye won't if
Ye take into con-si-der-ation
What dangers attend elevation!
The Priest—who expects him to descant
On duty with more zeal and less cant?
He preaches but rubbish he 's reared in.
The Soldier, grown deaf (by the mere din
Of battle) to mercy, learned tippling
And what not of vice while a stripling.
The Lawyer—his lies are conventional.
And as for the Poor Sort—why mention all
Obstructions that leave barred and bolted
Access to the brains of each dolt-head?"

He ended, you wager? Not half! A bet?
Precedence to males in the alphabet!
Still, disposed of Man's A B C, there 's X
Y Z want assistance,—the Fair Sex!
How much may be said in excuse of
Those vanities—males see no use of—
From silk shoe on heel to laced poll's-hood!
What 's their frailty beside our own falsehood?
The boldest, most brazen of ... trumpets,
How kind can they be to their dumb pets!
Of their charms—how are most frank, how few venal!
While as for those charges of Juvenal—

Quæ nemo dixisset in toto
Nisi (ædepol) ore illoto—
He dismissed every charge with an "Apage!"

X

Then, cocking (in Scotch phrase) his cap a-gee,
Right hand disengaged from the doublet
—Like landlord, in house he had sublet
Resuming of guardianship gestion,
To call tenants' conduct in question—
Hop, skip, jump, to inside from outside
Of chamber, he lords, ladies, louts eyed
With such transformation of visage
As fitted the censor of this age.
No longer an advocate tepid
Of frailty, but champion intrepid
Of strength,—not of falsehood but verity,—
He, one after one, with asperity
Stripped bare all the cant-clothed abuses,
Disposed of sophistic excuses,
Forced folly each shift to abandon,
And left vice with no leg to stand on.
So crushing the force he exerted,
That Man at his foot lay converted!

XI

True—Man bred of paint-pot and mortar!
But why suppose folks of this sort are
More likely to hear and be tractable
Than folks all alive and, in fact, able
To testify promptly by action
Their ardor, and make satisfaction
For misdeeds non verbis sed factis?
"With folks all alive be my practice
Henceforward! O mortar, paint-pot O,
Farewell to ye!" cried Pacchiarotto,
"Let only occasion intérpose!"

XII

It did so: for, pat to the purpose
Through causes I need not examine,
There fell upon Siena a famine.

In vain did the magistrates busily
Seek succor, fetch grain out of Sicily,
Nay, throw mill and bakehouse wide open—
Such misery followed as no pen
Of mine shall depict ye. Faint, fainter
Waxed hope of relief: so, our painter,
Emboldened by triumph of recency,
How could he do other with decency
Than rush in this strait to the rescue,
Play schoolmaster, point as with fescue
To each and all slips in Man's spelling
The law of the land?—slips now telling
With monstrous effect on the city,
Whose magistrates moved him to pity
As, bound to read law to the letter,
They minded their hornbook, no better.

XIII

I ought to have told you, at starting,
How certain, who itched to be carting
Abuses away clean and thorough
From Siena, both province and borough,
Had formed themselves into a company
Whose swallow could bolt in a lump any
Obstruction of scruple, provoking
The nicer throat's coughing and choking:
Fit Club, by as fit a name dignified
Of "Freed Ones"—"Bardotti"—which signified
"Spare-Horses" that walk by the wagon
The team has to drudge for and drag on.
This notable Club Pacchiarotto
Had joined long since, paid scot and lot to,
As free and accepted "Bardotto."
The Bailiwick watched with no quiet eye
The outrage thus done to society,
And noted the advent especially
Of Pacchiarotto their fresh ally.

XIV

These Spare-Horses forthwith assembled:
Neighed words whereat citizens trembled
As oft as the chiefs, in the Square by
The Duomo, proposed a way whereby
The city were cured of disaster.

"Just substitute servant for master,
Make Poverty Wealth and Wealth Poverty,
Unloose Man from overt and covert tie,
And straight out of social confusion
True Order would spring!" Brave illusion—
Aims heavenly attained by means earthy!

XV

Off to these at full speed rushed our worthy,—
Brain practised and tongue no less tutored,
In argument's armor accoutred,—
Sprang forth, mounted rostrum, and essayed
Proposals like those to which "Yes" said
So glibly each personage painted
O' the wall-side where with you 're acquainted.
He harangued on the faults of the Bailiwick:
"Red soon were our State-candle's paly wick,
If wealth would become but interfluous,
Fill voids up with just the superfluous;
If ignorance gave way to knowledge
—Not pedantry picked up at college
From Doctors, Professors et cætera—
(They say: 'kai ta loipa'—like better a
Long Greek string of kappas, taus, lambdas,
Tacked on to the tail of each damned ass)—
No knowledge we want of this quality,
But knowledge indeed—practicality
Through insight's fine universality!
If you shout 'Bailiffs, out on ye all! Fie,
Thou Chief of our forces, Amalfi,
Who shieldest the rogue and the clotpoll!'
If you pounce on and poke out, with what pole
I leave ye to fancy, our Siena's
Beast-litter of sloths and hyenas—"
(Whoever to scan this is ill able
Forgets the town's name 's a dissyllable)—
"If, this done, ye did—as ye might—place
For once the right man in the right place,
If you listened to me" ...

XVI

At which last "If"
There flew at his throat like a mastiff
One Spare-Horse—another and another!

Such outbreak of tumult and pother,
Horse-faces a-laughing and fleering,
Horse-voices a-mocking and jeering,
Horse-hands raised to collar the caitiff
Whose impudence ventured the late "If"—
That, had not fear sent Pacchiarotto
Off tramping, as fast as could trot toe,
Away from the scene o£ discomfiture—
Had he stood there stock-still in a dumb fit—sure
Am I he had paid in his person
Till his mother might fail to know her son,
Though she gazed on him never so wistful,
In the figure so tattered and tristful.
Each mouth full of curses, each fist full
Of cuffings—behold, Pacchiarotto,
The pass which thy project has got to,
Of trusting, nigh ashes still hot—tow!
(The paraphrase—which I much need—is
From Horace "per ignes incedis.")

XVII

Right and left did he dash helter-skelter
In agonized search of a shelter.
No purlieu so blocked and no alley
So blind as allowed him to rally
His spirits and see—nothing hampered
His steps if he trudged and not scampered
Up here and down there in a city
That 's all ups and downs, more the pity
For folks who would outrun the constable.
At last he stopped short at the one stable
And sure place of refuge that 's offered
Humanity. Lately was coffered
A corpse in its sepulchre, situate
By St. John's Observance. "Habituate
Thyself to the strangest of bedfellows,
And, kicked by the live, kiss the dead fellows!"
So Misery counselled the craven.
At once he crept safely to haven
Through a hole left unbricked in the structure.
Ay, Misery, in have you tucked your
Poor client and left him conterminous
With—pah!—the thing fetid and verminous!
(I gladly would spare you the detail,
But History writes what I retail.)

XVIII

Two days did he groan in his domicile:
"Good Saints, set me free and I promise I 'll
Abjure all ambition of preaching
Change, whether to minds touched by teaching
—The smooth folk of fancy, mere figments
Created by plaster and pigments,—
Or to minds that receive with such rudeness
Dissuasion from pride, greed and lewdness,
—The rough folk of fact, life's true specimens
Of mind—'hand in posse sed esse mens'
As it was, is, and shall be forever
Despite of my utmost endeavor.
O live foes I thought to illumine,
Henceforth lie untroubled your gloom in!
I need my own light, every spark, as
I couch with this sole friend—a carcase!"

XIX

Two days thus he maundered and rambled;
Then, starved back to sanity, scrambled
From out his receptacle loathsome.
"A spectre!"—declared upon oath some
Who saw him emerge and (appalling
To mention) his garments a-crawling
With plagues far beyond the Egyptian.
He gained, in a state past description,
A convent of months, the Observancy.

XX

Thus far is a fact: I reserve fancy
For Fancy's more proper employment:
And now she waves wing with enjoyment,
To tell ye how preached the Superior,
When somewhat our painter's exterior
Was sweetened. He needed (no mincing
The matter) much soaking and rinsing,
Nay, rubbing with drugs odoriferous,
Till, rid of his garments pestiferous,
And, robed by the help of the Brotherhood
In odds and ends,—this gown and t' other hood,—
His empty inside first well-garnished,—

He delivered a tale round, unvarnished.

XXI

"Ah, Youth!" ran the Abbot's admonishment,
"Thine error scarce moves my astonishment.
For—why shall I shrink from asserting?—
Myself have had hopes of converting
The foolish to wisdom, till, sober,
My life found its May grow October.
I talked and I wrote, but, one morning,
Life's Autumn bore fruit in this warning:
'Let tongue rest, and quiet thy quill be!
Earth is earth and not heaven, and ne'er will be.'
Man's work is to labor and leaven—
As best he may—earth here with heaven;
'T is work for work's sake that he 's needing:
Let, him work on and on as if speeding
Work's end, but not dream of succeeding!
Because if success were intended,
Why, heaven would begin ere earth ended.
A Spare-Horse? Be rather a thill-horse,
Or—what 's the plain truth—just a mill-horse!
Earth 's a mill where we grind and wear mufflers:
A whip awaits shirkers and shufflers
Who slacken their pace, sick of lugging
At what don't advance for their tugging.
Though round goes the mill, we must still post
On and on as if moving the mill-post.
So, grind away, mouth-wise and pen-wise,
Do all that we can to make men wise!
And if men prefer to be foolish,
Ourselves have proved horse-like not mulish:
Sent grist, a good sackful, to hopper,
And worked as the Master thought proper.
Tongue I wag, pen I ply, who am Abbot;
Stick, thou, Son, to daub-brush and dab-pot!
But, soft! I scratch hard on the scab hot?
Though cured of thy plague, there may linger
A pimple I fray with rough finger?
So soon could my homily transmute
Thy brass into gold? Why, the man 's mute!"

XXII

"Ay, Father, I 'm mute with admiring

How Nature's indulgence untiring
Still bids us turn deaf ear to Reason's
Best rhetoric—clutch at all seasons
And hold fast to what 's proved untenable!
Thy maxim is—Man 's not amenable
To argument: whereof by consequence—
Thine arguments reach me: a non-sequence!
Yet blush not discouraged, O Father!
I stand unconverted, the rather
That nowise I need a conversion.
No live man (I cap thy assertion)
By argument ever could take hold
Of me. 'T was the dead thing, the clay-cold,
Which grinned 'Art thou so in a hurry
That out of warm light thou must scurry
And join me down here in the dungeon
Because, above, one 's Jack and one—John,
One 's swift in the race, one—a hobbler,
One 's a crowned king and one—a capped cobbler,
Rich and poor, sage and fool, virtuous, vicious?
Why complain? Art thou so unsuspicious
That all 's for an hour of essaying
Who 's fit and who 's unfit for playing
His part in the after-construction
—Heaven's Piece whereof Earth 's the Induction?
Things rarely go smooth at Rehearsal.
Wait patient the change universal,
And act, and let act, in existence!
For, as thou art clapped hence or hissed hence,
Thou hast thy promotion or otherwise.
And why must wise thou have thy brother wise
Because in rehearsal thy cue be
To shine by the side of a booby?
No polishing garnet to ruby!
All 's well that ends well—through Art's magic.
Some end, whether comic or tragic,
The Artist has purposed, be certain!
Explained at the fall of the curtain—
In showing thy wisdom at odds with
That folly: he tries men and gods with
No problem for weak wits to solve meant,
But one worth such Author's evolvement.
So, back nor disturb play's production
By giving thy brother instruction
To throw up his fool's-part allotted!
Lest haply thyself prove besotted
When stript, for thy pains, of that costume
Of sage, which has bred the imposthume

I prick to relieve thee of,—Vanity!'

XXIII

"So, Father, behold me in sanity!
I 'm back to the palette and mahlstick:
And as for Man—let each and all stick
To what was prescribed them at starting!
Once planted as fools—no departing
From folly one inch, sæculorum
In sæcula! Pass me the jorum,
And push me the platter—my stomach
Retains, through its fasting, still some ache—
And then, with your kind Benedicite,
Good-by!"

XXIV

I have told with simplicity
My tale, dropped those harsh analytics,
And tried to content you, my critics,
Who greeted my early uprising!
I knew you through all the disguising,
Droll dogs, as I jumped up, cried "Heyday!
This Monday is—what else but May-day?
And these in the drabs, blues, and yellows,
Are surely the privileged fellows.
So, saltbox and bones, tongs and bellows!"
(I threw up the window) "Your pleasure?"

XXV

Then he who directed the measure—
An old friend—put leg forward nimbly,
"We critics as sweeps out your chimbly!
Much soot to remove from your flue, sir!
Who spares coal in kitchen an't you, sir!
And neighbors complain it 's no joke, sir,
—You ought to consume your own smoke, sir!"

XXVI

Ah, rogues, but my housemaid suspects you—
Is confident oft she detects you

In bringing more filth into my house
Than ever you found there! I 'm pious,
However: 't was God made you dingy
And me—with no need to be stingy
Of soap, when 't is sixpence the packet.
So, dance away, boys, dust my jacket,
Bang drum and blow fife—ay, and rattle
Your brushes, for that 's half the battle!
Don't trample the grass,—hocus-pocus
With grime my Spring snowdrop and crocus,—
And, what with your rattling and tinkling,
Who knows but you give me an inkling
How music sounds, thanks to the jangle
Of regular drum and triangle?
Whereby, tap-tap, chink-chink, 't is proven
I break rule as bad as Beethoven.
"That chord now—a groan or a grunt is 't?
Schumann's self was no worse contrapuntist.
No ear! or if ear, so tough-gristled—
He thought that he sung while he whistled!"

XXVII

So, this time I whistle, not sing at all,
My story, the largess I fling at all
And every the rough there whose aubade
Did its best to amuse me,—nor so bad!
Take my thanks, pick up largess, and scamper
Off free, ere your mirth gets a damper!
You 've Monday, your one day, your fun-day,
While mine is a year that 's all Sunday.
I 've seen you, times—who knows how many?—
Dance in here, strike up, play the zany,
Make mouths at the Tenant, hoot warning
You 'll find him decamped next May-morning;
Then scuttle away, glad to 'scape hence
With—kicks? no, but laughter and ha'pence!
Mine 's freehold, by grace of the grand Lord
Who lets out the ground here,—my landlord:
To him I pay quit-rent—devotion;
Nor hence shall I budge, I 've a notion,
Nay, here shall my whistling and singing
Set all his street's echoes a-ringing
Long after the last of your number
Has ceased my front-court to encumber
While, treading down rose and ranunculus,
You Tommy-make-room-for-your-Uncle us!

Troop, all of you—man or homunculus,
Quick march! for Xanthippe, my housemaid,
If once on your pates she a souse made
With what, pan or pot, bowl or skoramis,
First comes to her hand—things were more amiss!
I would not for worlds be your place in—
Recipient of slops from the basin!
You, Jack-in-the-Green, leaf-and-twiggishness
Won't save a dry thread on your priggishness!
While as for Quilp-Hop-o'-my-thumb there,
Banjo-Byron that twangs the strum-strum there—
He 'll think as the pickle he curses,
I 've discharged on his pate his own verses!
"Dwarfs are saucy," says Dickens: so, sauced in
Your own sauce, ...

XXVIII

But, back to my Knight of the Pencil,
Dismissed to his fresco and stencil!
Whose story—begun with a chuckle,
And throughout timed by raps of the knuckle,—
To small enough purpose were studied
If it ends with crown cracked or nose bloodied.
Come, critics,—not shake hands, excuse me!
But—say have you grudged to amuse me
This once in the forty-and-over
Long years since you trampled my clover
And scared from my house-eaves each sparrow
I never once harmed by that arrow
Of song, karterotaton belos,
(Which Pindar declares the true melos,)
I was forging and filing and finishing,
And no whit my labors diminishing
Because, though high up in a chamber
Where none of your kidney may clamber
Your hullabaloo would approach me?
Was it "grammar" wherein you would "coach" me—
You,—pacing in even that paddock
Of language allotted you ad hoc,
With a clog at your fetlocks,—you—scorners
Of me free of all its four corners?
Was it "clearness of words which convey thought"?
Ay, if words never needed enswathe aught
But ignorance, impudence, envy
And malice—what word-swathe would then vie
With yours for a clearness crystalline?

But had you to put in one small line
Some thought big and bouncing—as noddle
Of goose, born to cackle and waddle
And bite at man's heel as goose-wont is,
Never felt plague its puny os frontis—
You 'd know, as you hissed, spat and sputtered,
Clear cackle is easily uttered!

XXIX

Lo, I 've laughed out my laugh on this mirth-day!
Beside, at week's end, dawns my birthday,
That hebdome, hieron emar—
(More things in a day than you deem are!)
—Tei gar Apollona chrusaora
Egeinato Leto. So, gray or ray
Betide me, six days hence, I 'm vexed here
By no sweep, that 's certain, till next year!
"Vexed?"—roused from what else were insipid ease!
Leave snoring abed to Pheidippides!
We 'll up and work! won't we, Euripides?

AT THE "MERMAID"

The figure that thou here seest ... Tut!
Was it for gentle Shakespeare put?
B. JONSON (Adapted)

I—"Next Poet?" No, my hearties,
I nor am nor fain would be!
Choose your chiefs and pick your parties,
Not one soul revolt to me!
I, forsooth, sow song-sedition?
I, a schism in verse provoke?
I, blown up by bard's ambition,
Burst—your bubble-king? You joke.

Come, be grave! The sherris mantling
Still about each mouth, mayhap,
Breeds you insight—just a scantling—
Brings me truth out—just a scrap.
Look and tell me! Written, spoken,
Here 's my life-long work: and where
—Where 's your warrant or my token
I 'm the dead king's son and heir?

Here 's my work: does work discover—
What was rest from work—my life?
Did I live man's hater, lover?
Leave the world at peace, at strife?
Call earth ugliness or beauty?
See things there in large or small?
Use to pay its Lord my duty?
Use to own a lord at all?

Blank of such a record, truly,
Here 's the work I hand, this scroll,
Yours to take or leave; as duly,
Mine remains the unproffered soul.
So much, no whit more, my debtors—
How should one like me lay claim
To that largess elders, betters
Sell you cheap their souls for—fame?

Which of you did I enable
Once to slip inside my breast,
There to catalogue and label
What I like least, what love best,
Hope and fear, believe and doubt of,
Seek and shun, respect—deride?
Who has right to make a rout of
Rarities he found inside?

Rarities or, as he 'd rather,
Rubbish such as stocks his own:
Need and greed (oh, strange) the Father
Fashioned not for him alone!
Whence—the comfort set a-strutting,
Whence—the outcry "Haste, behold!
Bard's breast open wide, past shutting,
Shows what brass we took for gold!"

Friends, I doubt not he 'd display you
Brass—myself call orichale,—
Furnish much amusement; pray you
Therefore, be content I balk
Him and you, and bar my portal!
Here 's my work outside: opine
What 's inside me mean and mortal!
Take your pleasure, leave me mine!

Which is—not to buy your laurel
As last king did, nothing loth.

Tale adorned and pointed moral
Gained him praise and pity both.
Out rushed sighs and groans by dozens,
Forth by scores oaths, curses flew:
Proving you were cater-cousins,
Kith and kindred, king and you!

Whereas do I ne'er so little
(Thanks to sherris), leave ajar
Bosom's gate—no jot nor tittle
Grow we nearer than we are.
Sinning, sorrowing, despairing,
Body-ruined, spirit-wrecked,—
Should I give my woes an airing,—
Where 's one plague that claims respect?

Have you found your life distasteful?
My life did and does smack sweet.
Was your youth of pleasure wasteful?
Mine I saved and hold complete.
Do your joys with age diminish?
When mine fail me, I 'll complain.
Must in death your daylight finish?
My sun sets to rise again.

What, like you, he proved—your Pilgrim—
This our world a wilderness,
Earth still gray and heaven still grim,
Not a hand there his might press,
Not a heart his own might throb to,
Men all rogues and women—say,
Dolls which boys' heads duck and bob to,
Grown folk drop or throw away?

My experience being other,
How should I contribute verse
Worthy of your king and brother?
Balaam-like I bless, not curse.
I find earth not gray but rosy,
Heaven not grim but fair of hue.
Do I stoop? I pluck a posy.
Do I stand and stare? All 's blue.

Doubtless I am pushed and shoved by
Rogues and fools enough: the more
Good luck mine, I love, am loved by
Some few honest to the core.
Scan the near high, scout the far low!

"But the low come close:" what then?
Simpletons? My match is Marlowe;
Sciolists? My mate is Ben.

Womankind—"the cat-like nature,
False and fickle, vain and weak"—
What of this sad nomenclature
Suits my tongue, if I must speak?
Does the sex invite, repulse so,
Tempt, betray, by fits and starts?
So becalm but to convulse so,
Decking heads and breaking hearts?

Well may you blaspheme at fortune!
I "threw Venus" (Ben, expound!)
Never did I need importune
Her, of all the Olympian round.
Blessings on my benefactress!
Cursings suit—for aught I know—
Those who twitched her by the back tress,
Tugged and thought to turn her—so!

Therefore, since no leg to stand on
Thus I 'm left with,—joy or grief
Be the issue,—I abandon
Hope or care you name me Chief!
Chief and king and Lord's anointed,
I?—who never once have wished
Death before the day appointed:
Lived and liked, not poohed and pished!

"Ah, but so I shall not enter,
Scroll in hand, the common heart—
Stopped at surface: since at centre
Song should reach Welt-schmerz, world-smart!"
"Enter in the heart?" Its shelly
Cuirass guard mine, fore and aft!
Such song "enters in the belly
And is cast out in the draught."

Back then to our sherris-brewage!
"Kingship" quotha? I shall wait—
Waive the present time: some new age ...
But let fools anticipate!
Meanwhile greet me—"friend, good fellow,
Gentle Will," my merry men!
As for making Envy yellow
With "Next Poet"—(Manners, Ben!)

HOUSE

Shall I sonnet-sing you about myself?
Do I live in a house you would like to see?
Is it scant of gear, has it store of pelf?
"Unlock my heart with a sonnet-key?"

Invite the world, as my betters have done?
"Take notice: this building remains on view,
Its suites of reception every one,
Its private apartment and bedroom too;

"For a ticket, apply to the Publisher."
No: thanking the public, I must decline.
A peep through my window, if folk prefer;
But, please you, no foot over threshold of mine!

I have mixed with a crowd and heard free talk
In a foreign land where an earthquake chanced
And a house stood gaping, naught to balk
Man's eye wherever he gazed or glanced.

The whole of the frontage shaven sheer,
The inside gaped: exposed to day,
Right and wrong and common and queer,
Bare, as the palm of your hand, it lay.

The owner? Oh, he had been crushed, no doubt!
"Odd tables and chairs for a man of wealth!
What a parcel of musty old books about!
He smoked,—no wonder he lost his health!

"I doubt if he bathed before he dressed.
A brasier?—the pagan, he burned perfumes!
You see it is proved, what the neighbors guessed:
His wife and himself had separate rooms."

Friends, the goodman of the house at least
Kept house to himself till an earthquake came:
'T is the fall of its frontage permits you feast
On the inside arrangement you praise or blame.

Outside should suffice for evidence:
And whoso desires to penetrate
Deeper, must dive by the spirit-sense—

No optics like yours, at any rate!

"Hoity-toity! A street to explore,
Your house the exception! 'With this same key
Shakespeare unlocked his heart,' once more!"
Did Shakespeare? If so, the less Shakespeare he!

SHOP

So, friend, your shop was all your house!
Its front, astonishing the street,
Invited view from man and mouse
To what diversity of treat
Behind its glass—the single sheet!

What gimcracks, genuine Japanese:
Gape-jaw and goggle-eye, the frog;
Dragons, owls, monkeys, beetles, geese;
Some crush-nosed human-hearted dog:
Queer names, too, such a catalogue!

I thought "And he who owns the wealth
Which blocks the window's vastitude,
—Ah, could I peep at him by stealth
Behind his ware, pass shop, intrude
On house itself, what scenes were viewed!

"If wide and showy thus the shop,
What must the habitation prove?
The true house with no name a-top—
The mansion, distant one remove,
Once get him off his traffic-groove!

"Pictures he likes, or books perhaps;
And as for buying most and best,
Commend me to these city chaps!
Or else he 's social, takes his rest
On Sundays, with a Lord for guest.

"Some suburb-palace, parked about
And gated grandly, built last year:
The four-mile walk to keep off gout;
Or big seat sold by bankrupt peer:
But then he takes the rail, that 's clear.

"Or, stop! I wager, taste selects

Some out-o'-the-way, some all-unknown
Retreat: the neighborhood suspects
Little that he who rambles lone
Makes Rothschild tremble on his throne!"

Nowise! Nor Mayfair residence
Fit to receive and entertain,—
Nor Hampstead villa's kind defence
From noise and crowd, from dust and drain,—
Nor country-box was soul's domain!

Nowise! At back of all that spread
Of merchandise, woe 's me, I find
A hole i' the wall where, heels by head,
The owner couched, his ware behind,
—In cupboard suited to his mind.

For why? He saw no use of life
But, while he drove a roaring trade,
To chuckle "Customers are rife!"
To chafe "So much hard cash outlaid,
Yet zero in my profits made!

"This novelty costs pains, but—takes?
Cumbers my counter! Stock no more!
This article, no such great shakes,
Fizzes like wildfire? Underscore
The cheap thing—thousands to the fore!"

'T was lodging best to live most nigh
(Cramp, coffinlike as crib might be)
Receipt of Custom; ear and eye
Wanted no outworld: "Hear and see
The bustle in the shop!" quoth he.

My fancy of a merchant-prince
Was different. Through his wares we groped
Our darkling way to—not to mince
The matter—no black den where moped
The master if we interloped!

Shop was shop only: household-stuff?
What did he want with comforts there?
"Walls, ceiling, floor, stay blank and rough,
So goods on sale show rich and rare!
'Sell and scud home,' be shop's affair!"

What might he deal in? Gems, suppose!

Since somehow business must be done
At cost of trouble,—see, he throws
You choice of jewels, every one,
Good, better, best, star, moon, and sun!

Which lies within your power of purse?
This ruby that would tip aright
Solomon's sceptre? Oh, your nurse
Wants simply coral, the delight
Of teething baby,—stuff to bite!

Howe'er your choice fell, straight you took
Your purchase, prompt your money rang
On counter,—scarce the man forsook
His study of the "Times," just swang
Till-ward his hand that stopped the clang,—

Then off made buyer with a prize,
Then seller to his "Times" returned;
And so did day wear, wear, till eyes
Brightened apace, for rest was earned:
He locked door long ere candle burned.

And whither went he? Ask himself,
Not me! To change of scene, I think.
Once sold the ware and pursed the pelf,
Chaffer was scarce his meat and drink,
Nor all his music—money-chink.

Because a man has shop to mind
In time and place, since flesh must live,
Needs spirit lack all life behind,
All stray thoughts, fancies fugitive,
All loves except what trade can give?

I want to know a butcher paints,
A baker rhymes for his pursuit,
Candlestick-maker much acquaints
His soul with song, or, haply mute,
Blows out his brains upon the flute!

But—shop each day and all day long!
Friend, your good angel slept, your star
Suffered eclipse, fate did you wrong!
From where these sorts of treasures are,
There should our hearts be—Christ, how far!

PISGAH-SIGHTS

When sanctioning a volume of Selections from his poems, Browning made a third of Pisgah-Sights to consist of the Proem to La Saisiaz.

I

Over the ball of it,
Peering and prying,
How I see all of it,
Life there, outlying!
Roughness and smoothness,
Shine and defilement,
Grace and uncouthness:
One reconcilement.

Orbed as appointed,
Sister with brother
Joins, ne'er disjointed
One from the other.
All 's lend-and-borrow;
Good, see, wants evil,
Joy demands sorrow,
Angel weds devil!

"Which things must—why be?"
Vain our endeavor!
So shall things aye be
As they were ever.
"Such things should so be!"
Sage our desistence!
Rough-smooth let globe be,
Mixed—man's existence!

Man—wise and foolish,
Lover and scorner,
Docile and mulish—
Keep each his corner!
Honey yet gall of it!
There 's the life lying,
And I see all of it,
Only, I 'm dying!

II

Could I but live again

Twice my life over,
Would I once strive again?
Would not I cover
Quietly all of it—
Greed and ambition—
So, from the pall of it,
Pass to fruition?

"Soft!" I 'd say, "Soul mine!
Three-score and ten years,
Let the blind mole mine
Digging out deniers!
Let the dazed hawk soar,
Claim the sun's rights too!
Turf 't is thy walk 's o'er,
Foliage thy flight 's to."

Only a learner,
Quick one or slow one,
Just a discerner,
I would teach no one.
I am earth's native:
No rearranging it!
I be creative,
Chopping and changing it?

March, men, my fellows!
Those who, above me,
(Distance so mellows)
Fancy you love me:
Those who, below me,
(Distance makes great so)
Free to forego me,
Fancy you hate so!

Praising, reviling,
Worst head and best head,
Past me defiling,
Never arrested,
Wanters, abounders,
March, in gay mixture,
Men, my surrounders!
I am the fixture.

So shall I fear thee,
Mightiness yonder!
Mock-sun—more near thee,
What is to wonder?

So shall I love thee,
Down in the dark,—lest
Glowworm I prove thee,
Star that now sparklest!

FEARS AND SCRUPLES

In answer to a letter of inquiry, addressed to him by Mr. W. G. Kingsland, Browning wrote the following in regard to the meaning of this poem: "I think, that the point I wanted to illustrate was this: Where there is a genuine love of the 'letters' and 'actions' of the invisible 'friend,'—however these may be disadvantaged by an inability to meet the objections to their authenticity or historical value urged by 'experts' who assume the privilege of learning over ignorance,—it would indeed be a wrong to the wisdom and goodness of the 'friend' if he were supposed capable of overlooking the actual 'love' and only considering the 'ignorance' which, failing to in any degree affect 'love,' is really the highest evidence that 'love' exists. So I meant, whether the result be clear or no."

Here's my case. Of old I used to love him,
This same unseen friend, before I knew:
Dream there was none like him, none above him,—
Wake to hope and trust my dream was true.

Loved I not his letters full of beauty?
Not his actions famous far and wide?
Absent, he would know I vowed him duty;
Present, he would find me at his side.

Pleasant fancy! for I had but letters,
Only knew of actions by hearsay:
He himself was busied with my betters;
What of that? My turn must come some day.

"Some day" proving—no day! Here 's the puzzle.
Passed and passed my turn is. Why complain?
He 's so busied! If I could but muzzle
People's foolish mouths that give me pain!

"Letters?" (hear them!) "You a judge of writing?
Ask the experts! How they shake the head
O'er these characters, your friend's inditing—
Call them forgery from A to Z!

"Actions? Where 's your certain proof" (they bother)
"He, of all you find so great and good,
He, he only, claims this, that, the other
Action—claimed by men, a multitude?"

I can simply-wish. I might refute you,
Wish my friend would,—by a word, a wink,—
Bid me stop that foolish mouth,—you brute you!
He keeps absent,—why, I cannot think.

Never mind! Though foolishness may flout me,
One thing 's sure enough: 't is neither frost,
No, nor fire, shall freeze or burn from out me
Thanks for truth—though falsehood, gained—though lost.

All my days, I 'll go the softlier, sadlier,
For that dream's sake! How forget the thrill
Through and through me as I thought "The gladlier
Lives my friend because I love him still!"

Ah, but there 's a menace some one utters!
"What and if your friend at home play tricks?
Peep at hide-and-seek behind the shutters?
Mean your eyes should pierce through solid bricks?

"What and if he, frowning, wake you, dreamy?
Lay on you the blame that bricks—conceal?
Say 'At least I saw who did not see me,
Does see now, and presently shall feel'?"

"Why, that makes your friend a monster!" say you:
"Had his house no window? At first nod,
Would you not have hailed him?" Hush, I pray you!
What if this friend happened to be—God?

NATURAL MAGIC

All I can say is—I saw it!
The room was as bare as your hand.
I locked in the swarth little lady,—I swear,
From the head to the foot of her—well, quite as bare!
"No Nautch shall cheat me," said I, "taking my stand
At this bolt which I draw!" And this bolt—I withdraw it,
And there laughs the lady, not bare, but embowered
With—who knows what verdure, o'erfruited, o'erflowered?
Impossible! Only—I saw it!

All I can sing is—I feel it!
This life was as blank as that room;
I let you pass in here. Precaution, indeed?
Walls, ceiling and floor,—not a chance for a weed!

Wide opens the entrance; where 's cold now, where 's gloom?
No May to sow seed here, no June to reveal it,
Behold you enshrined in these blooms of your bringing,
These fruits of your bearing—nay, birds of your winging!
A fairy-tale! Only—I feel it!

MAGICAL NATURE

Flower—I never fancied, jewel—I profess you!
Bright I see and soft I feel the outside of a flower.
Save but glow inside and—jewel, I should guess you,
Dim to sight and rough to touch: the glory is the dower.

You, forsooth, a flower? Nay, my love, a jewel—
Jewel at no mercy of a moment in your prime!
Time may fray the flower-face: kind be time or cruel,
Jewel, from each facet, flash your laugh at time!

BIFURCATION

We were two lovers; let me lie by her,
My tomb beside her tomb. On hers inscribe—
"I loved him; but my reason bade prefer
Duty to love, reject the tempter's bribe
Of rose and lily when each path diverged,
And either I must pace to life's far end
As love should lead me, or, as duty urged,
Plod the worn causeway arm-in-arm with friend.
So, truth turned falsehood: 'How I loathe a flower,
How prize the pavement!' still caressed his ear—
The deafish friend's—through life's day, hour by hour,
As he laughed (coughing) 'Ay, it would appear!'
But deep within my heart of hearts there hid
Ever the confidence, amends for all,
That heaven repairs what wrong earth's journey did,
When love from life-long exile comes at call.
Duty and love, one broad way, were the best—
Who doubts? But one or other was to choose,
I chose the darkling half, and wait the rest
In that new world where light and darkness fuse."

Inscribe on mine—"I loved her: love's track lay
O'er sand and pebble, as all travellers know.
Duty led through a smiling country, gay

With greensward where the rose and lily blow.
'Our roads are diverse: farewell, love!' said she:
"'T is duty I abide by: homely sward
And not the rock-rough picturesque for me!
Above, where both roads join, I wait reward.
Be you as constant to the path whereon
I leave you planted!' But man needs must move,
Keep moving—whither, when the star is gone
Whereby he steps secure nor strays from love?
No stone but I was tripped by, stumbling-block
But brought me to confusion. Where I fell,
There I lay flat, if moss disguised the rock,
Thence, if flint pierced, I rose and cried 'All's well!
Duty be mine to tread in that high sphere
Where love from duty ne'er disparts, I trust,
And two halves make that whole, whereof—since here
One must suffice a man—why, this one must!'"

Inscribe each tomb thus: then, some sage acquaint
The simple—which holds sinner, which holds saint!

NUMPHOLEPTOS

The Browning Society became so puzzled over the interpretation of this poem that through Dr. Furnivall it applied to the poet for an explanation and he replied: "Is not the key to the meaning of the poem in its title νυμφόληπτος [caught or rapt by a nymph] not γυναικεραστής [a woman lover]? An allegory, that is, of an impossible ideal object of love, accepted conventionally as such by a man who, all the while, cannot quite blind himself to the demonstrable fact that the possessor of knowledge and purity obtained without the natural consequences of obtaining them by achievement—not inheritance,—such a being is imaginary, not real, a nymph and no woman; and only such an one would be ignorant of and surprised at the results of a lover's endeavor to emulate the qualities which the beloved is entitled to consider as pre-existent to earthly experience, and independent of its inevitable results. I had no particular woman in my mind; certainly never intended to personify wisdom, philosophy, or any other abstraction; and the orb, raying color out of whiteness, was altogether a fancy of my own. The 'seven spirits' are in the Apocalypse, also in Coleridge and Byron,—a common image."

Still you stand, still you listen, still you smile!
Still melts your moonbeam through me, white awhile,
Softening, sweetening, till sweet and soft
Increase so round this heart of mine, that oft
I could believe your moonbeam-smile has past
The pallid limit, lies, transformed at last
To sunlight and salvation—warms the soul
It sweetens, softens! Would you pass that goal,
Gain love's birth at the limit's happier verge,
And, where an iridescence lurks, but urge

The hesitating pallor on to prime
Of dawn!—true blood-streaked, sun-warmth, action-time,
By heart-pulse ripened to a ruddy glow
Of gold above my clay—I scarce should know
From gold's self, thus suffused! For gold means love.
What means the sad slow silver smile above
My clay but pity, pardon?—at the best,
But acquiescence that I take my rest,
Contented to be clay, while in your heaven
The sun reserves love for the Spirit-Seven
Companioning God's throne they lamp before,
—Leaves earth a mute waste only wandered o'er
By that pale soft sweet disempassioned moon
Which smiles me slow forgiveness! Such, the boon
I beg? Nay, dear, submit to this—just this
Supreme endeavor! As my lips now kiss
Your feet, my arms convulse your shrouding robe,
My eyes, acquainted with the dust, dare probe
Your eyes above for—what, if born, would blind
Mine with redundant bliss, as flash may find
The inert nerve, sting awake the palsied limb,
Bid with life's ecstasy sense overbrim
And suck back death in the resurging joy—
Love, the love whole and sole without alloy!

Vainly! The promise withers! I employ
Lips, arms, eyes, pray the prayer which finds the word,
Make the appeal which must be felt, not heard,
And none the more is changed your calm regard:
Rather, its sweet and soft grow harsh, and hard—
Forbearance, then repulsion, then disdain.
Avert the rest! I rise, see!—make, again
Once more, the old departure for some track
Untried, yet through a world which brings me back
Ever thus fruitlessly to find your feet,
To fix your eyes, to pray the soft and sweet
Which smile there—take from his new pilgrimage
Your outcast, once your inmate, and assuage
With love—not placid pardon now—his thirst
For a mere drop from out the ocean erst
He drank at! Well, the quest shall be renewed.
Fear nothing! Though I linger, unembued
With any drop, my lips thus close. I go!
So did I leave you, I have found you so,
And doubtlessly, if fated to return,
So shall my pleading persevere and earn
Pardon—not love—in that same smile, I learn,
And lose the meaning of, to learn once more,

Vainly!

What fairy track do I explore?
What magic hall return to, like the gem
Centuply-angled o'er a diadem?
You dwell there, hearted; from your midmost home
Rays forth—through that fantastic world I roam
Ever—from centre to circumference,
Shaft upon colored shaft: this crimsons thence,
That purples out its precinct through the waste.
Surely I had your sanction when I faced,
Fared forth upon that untried yellow ray
Whence I retrack my steps? They end to-day
Where they began, before your feet, beneath
Your eyes, your smile: the blade is shut in sheath,
Fire quenched in flint; irradiation, late
Triumphant through the distance, finds its fate,
Merged in your blank pure soul, alike the source
And tomb of that prismatic glow: divorce
Absolute, all-conclusive! Forth I fared,
Treading the lambent flamelet: little cared
If now its flickering took the topaz tint,
If now my dull-caked path gave sulphury hint
Of subterranean rage—no stay nor stint
To yellow, since you sanctioned that I bathe,
Burnish me, soul and body, swim and swathe
In yellow license. Here I reek suffused
With crocus, saffron, orange, as I used
With scarlet, purple, every dye o' the bow
Born of the storm-cloud. As before, you show
Scarce recognition, no approval, some
Mistrust, more wonder at a man become
Monstrous in garb, nay—flesh disguised as well,
Through his adventure. Whatsoe'er befell,
I followed, wheresoe'er it wound, that vein
You authorized should leave your whiteness, stain
Earth's sombre stretch beyond your midmost place
Of vantage,—trode that tinct whereof the trace
On garb and flesh repel you! Yes, I plead
Your own permission—your command, indeed,
That who would worthily retain the love
Must share the knowledge shrined those eyes above,
Go boldly on adventure, break through bounds
O' the quintessential whiteness that surrounds
Your feet, obtain experience of each tinge
That bickers forth to broaden out, impinge
Plainer his foot its pathway all distinct
From every other. Ah, the wonder, linked

With fear, as exploration manifests
What agency it was first tipped the crests
Of unnamed wildflower, soon protruding grew
Portentous 'mid the sands, as when his hue
Betrays him and the burrowing snake gleams through;
Till, last ... but why parade more shame and pain?
Are not the proofs upon me? Here again
I pass into your presence, I receive
Your smile of pity, pardon, and I leave ...
No, not this last of times I leave you, mute,
Submitted to my penance, so my foot
May yet again adventure, tread, from source
To issue, one more ray of rays which course
Each other, at your bidding, from the sphere
Silver and sweet, their birthplace, down that drear
Dark of the world,—you promise shall return
Your pilgrim jewelled as with drops o' the urn
The rainbow paints from, and no smatch at all
Of ghastliness at edge of some cloud-pall
Heaven cowers before, as earth awaits the fall
O' the bolt and flash of doom. Who trusts your word
Tries the adventure: and returns—absurd
As frightful—in that sulphur-steeped disguise
Mocking the priestly cloth-of-gold, sole prize
The arch-heretic was wont to bear away
Until he reached the burning. No, I say:
No fresh adventure! No more seeking love
At end of toil, and finding, calm above
My passion, the old statuesque regard,
The sad petrific smile!

O you—less hard
And hateful than mistaken and obtuse
Unreason of a she-intelligence!
You very woman with the pert pretence
To match the male achievement! Like enough!
Ay, you were easy victors, did the rough
Straightway efface itself to smooth, the gruff
Grind down and grow a whisper,—did man's truth
Subdue, for sake of chivalry and ruth,
Its rapier-edge to suit the bulrush-spear
Womanly falsehood fights with! O that ear
All fact pricks rudely, that thrice-superfine
Feminity of sense, with right divine
To waive all process, take result stain-free
From out the very muck wherein ...

Ah me!

The true slave's querulous outbreak! All the rest
Be resignation! Forth at your behest
I fare. Who knows but this—the crimson-quest—
May deepen to a sunrise, not decay
To that cold sad sweet smile?—which I obey.

APPEARANCES

And so you found that poor room dull,
Dark, hardly to your taste, my dear?
Its features seemed unbeautiful:
But this I know—'t was there, not here,
You plighted troth to me, the word
Which—ask that poor room how it heard.

And this rich room obtains your praise
Unqualified,—so bright, so fair,
So all whereat perfection stays?
Ay, but remember—here, not there,
The other word was spoken!—Ask
This rich room how you dropped the mask!

ST. MARTIN'S SUMMER

No protesting, dearest!
Hardly kisses even!
Don't we both know how it ends?
How the greenest leaf turns serest,
Bluest outbreak—blankest heaven,
Lovers—friends?

You would build a mansion,
I would weave a bower
—Want the heart for enterprise.
Walls admit of no expansion:
Trellis-work may haply flower
Twice the size.

What makes glad Life's Winter?
New buds, old blooms after.
Sad the sighing "How suspect
Beams would ere mid-Autumn splinter,
Rooftree scarce support a rafter,
Walls lie wrecked?"

You are young, my princess!
I am hardly older:
Yet—I steal a glance behind!
Dare I tell you what convinces
Timid me that you, if bolder,
Bold—are blind?

Where we plan our dwelling
Glooms a graveyard surely!
Headstone, footstone moss may drape,—
Name, date, violets hide from spelling,—
But, though corpses rot obscurely,
Ghosts escape.

Ghosts! O breathing Beauty,
Give my frank word pardon!
What if I—somehow, somewhere—
Pledged my soul to endless duty
Many a time and oft? Be hard on
Love—laid there?

Nay, blame grief that 's fickle,
Time that proves a traitor,
Chance, change, all that purpose warps,—
Death who spares to thrust the sickle
Laid Love low, through flowers which later
Shroud the corpse!

And you, my winsome lady,
Whisper with like frankness!
Lies nothing buried long ago?
Are yon—which shimmer 'mid the shady
Where moss and violet run to rankness—
Tombs or no?

Who taxes you with murder?
My hands are clean—or nearly!
Love being mortal needs must pass.
Repentance? Nothing were absurder.
Enough: we felt Love's loss severely;
Though now—alas!

Love's corpse lies quiet therefore,
Only Love's ghost plays truant,
And warns us have in wholesome awe
Durable mansionry; that's wherefore
I weave but trellis-work, pursuant

—Life, to law.

The solid, not the fragile,
Tempts rain and hail and thunder.
If bower stand firm at Autumn's close,
Beyond my hope,—why, boughs were agile;
If bower fall flat, we scarce need wonder
Wreathing—rose!

So, truce to the protesting,
So, muffled be the kisses!
For, would we but avow the truth,
Sober is genuine joy. No jesting!
Ask else Penelope, Ulysses—
Old in youth!

For why should ghosts feel angered?
Let all their interference
Be faint march-music in the air!
"Up! Join the rear of us the vanguard!
Up, lovers, dead to all appearance,
Laggard pair!"

The while you clasp me closer,
The while I press you deeper,
As safe we chuckle,—under breath,
Yet all the slyer, the jocoser,—
"So, life can boast its day, like leap-year,
Stolen from death!"

Ah me—the sudden terror!
Hence quick—avaunt, avoid me,
You cheat, the ghostly flesh-disguised!
Nay, all the ghosts in one! Strange error!
So, 't was Death's self that clipped and coyed me,
Loved—and lied!

Ay, dead loves are the potent!
Like any cloud they used you,
Mere semblance you, but substance they!
Build we no mansion, weave we no tent!
Mere flesh—their spirit interfused you!
Hence, I say!

All theirs, none yours the glamour!
Theirs each low word that won me,
Soft look that found me Love's, and left
What else but you—the tears and clamor

That 's all your very own! Undone me—
Ghost-bereft!

HERVÉ RIEL

This ballad was printed first in the Cornhill Magazine for March, 1871. In a letter to Mr. George Smith, one of the publishers of the magazine, Browning stated that he intended to devote the proceeds of the poem to the aid of the people of Paris suffering from the Franco-German war. The publisher generously seconded his resolve and paid one hundred pounds for the poem.

I

On the sea and at the Hogue, sixteen hundred ninety-two,
Did the English fight the French,—woe to France!
And, the thirty-first of May, helter-skelter through the blue,
Like a crowd of frightened porpoises a shoal of sharks pursue,
Came crowding ship on ship to Saint Malo on the Rance,
With the English fleet in view.

II

'T was the squadron that escaped, with the victor in full chase;
First and foremost of the drove, in his great ship, Damfreville;
Close on him fled, great and small,
Twenty-two good ships in all;
And they signalled to the place
"Help the winners of a race!
Get us guidance, give us harbor, take us quick—or, quicker still,
Here 's the English can and will!"

III

Then the pilots of the place put out brisk and leapt on board;
"Why, what hope or chance have ships like these to pass?" laughed they:
"Rocks to starboard, rocks to port, all the passage scarred and scored,
Shall the 'Formidable' here with her twelve and eighty guns
Think to make the river-mouth by the single narrow way,
Trust to enter where 't is ticklish for a craft of twenty tons,
And with flow at full beside?
Now, 't is slackest ebb of tide.
Reach the mooring? Rather say,
While rock stands or water runs,
Not a ship will leave the bay!"

IV

Then was called a council straight.
Brief and bitter the debate:
"Here 's the English at our heels; would you have them take in tow
All that 's left us of the fleet, linked together stern and bow,
For a prize to Plymouth Sound?
Better run the ships aground!"
(Ended Damfreville his speech).
"Not a minute more to wait!
Let the Captains all and each
Shove ashore, then blow up, burn the vessels on the beach!
France must undergo her fate.

V

"Give the word!" But no such word
Was ever spoke or heard;
For up stood, for out stepped, for in struck amid all these
—A Captain? A Lieutenant? A Mate—first, second, third?
No such man of mark, and meet
With his betters to compete!
But a simple Breton sailor pressed by Tourville for the fleet,
A poor coasting-pilot he, Hervé Riel the Croisickese.

VI

And "What mockery or malice have we here?" cries Hervé Riel:
"Are you mad, you Malouins? Are you cowards, fools, or rogues?
Talk to me of rocks and shoals, me who took the soundings, tell
On my fingers every bank, every shallow, every swell
'Twixt the offing here and Grève where the river disembogues?
Are you bought by English gold? Is it love the lying 's for?
Morn and eve, night and day,
Have I piloted your bay,
Entered free and anchored fast at the foot of Solidor.
Burn the fleet and ruin France? That were worse than fifty Hogues!
Sirs, they know I speak the truth! Sirs, believe me there 's a way!
Only let me lead the line,
Have the biggest ship to steer,
Get this 'Formidable' clear,
Make the others follow mine,
And I lead them, most and least, by a passage I know well,
Right to Solidor past Grève,
And there lay them safe and sound;

And if one ship misbehave,
—Keel so much as grate the ground,
Why, I 've nothing but my life,—here 's my head!" cries Hervé Riel.

Not a minute more to wait.
"Steer us in, then, small and great!
Take the helm, lead the line, save the squadron!" cried its chief.
Captains, give the sailor place!
He is Admiral, in brief.
Still the north-wind, by God's grace!
See the noble fellow's face
As the big ship, with a bound,
Clears the entry like a hound,
Keeps the passage as its inch of way were the wide sea's profound!
See, safe through shoal and rock,
How they follow in a flock,
Not a ship that misbehaves, not a keel that grates the ground,
Not a spar that comes to grief!
The peril, see, is past,
All are harbored to the last,
And just as Hervé Riel hollas "Anchor!"—sure as fate,
Up the English come—too late!

So, the storm subsides to calm:
They see the green trees wave
On the heights o'erlooking Grève.
Hearts that bled are stanched with balm.
"Just our rapture to enhance,
Let the English rake the bay,
Gnash their teeth and glare askance
As they cannonade away!
'Neath rampired Solidor pleasant riding on the Rance!"
How hope succeeds despair on each Captain's countenance!
Out burst all with one accord,
"This is Paradise for Hell!
Let France, let France's King
Thank the man that did the thing!"
What a shout, and all one word,
"Hervé Riel!"
As he stepped in front once more,
Not a symptom of surprise
In the frank blue Breton eyes,

Just the same man as before.

IX

Then said Damfreville, "My friend,
I must speak out at the end,
Though I find the speaking hard.
Praise is deeper than the lips:
You have saved the King his ships,
You must name your own reward.
'Faith, our sun was near eclipse!
Demand whate'er you will,
France remains your debtor still.
Ask to heart's content and have! or my name 's not Damfreville."

X

Then a beam of fun outbroke
On the bearded mouth that spoke,
As the honest heart laughed through
Those frank eyes of Breton blue:
"Since I needs must say my say,
Since on board the duty 's done.
And from Malo Roads to Croisic Point, what is it but a run?—
Since 't is ask and have, I may—
Since the others go ashore—
Come! A good whole holiday!
Leave to go and see my wife, whom I call the Belle Aurore!"
That he asked and that he got,—nothing more.

XI

Name and deed alike are lost:
Not a pillar nor a post
In his Croisic keeps alive the feat as it befell;
Not a head in white and black
On a single fishing-smack,
In memory of the man but for whom had gone to wrack
All that France saved from the fight whence England bore the bell.
Go to Paris: rank on rank
Search the heroes flung pell-mell
On the Louvre, face and flank!
You shall look long enough ere you come to Hervé Riel.
So, for better and for worse,
Hervé Riel, accept my verse!

In my verse, Hervé Riel, do thou once more
Save the squadron, honor France, love thy wife the Belle Aurore!

A FORGIVENESS

I am indeed the personage you know.
As for my wife,—what happened long ago—
You have a right to question me, as I
Am bound to answer.

("Son, a fit reply!"
The monk half spoke, half ground through his clenched teeth,
At the confession-grate I knelt beneath.)

Thus then all happened, Father! Power and place
I had as still I have. I ran life's race,
With the whole world to see, as only strains
His strength some athlete whose prodigious gains
Of good appall him: happy to excess,—
Work freely done should balance happiness
Fully enjoyed; and, since beneath my roof
Housed she who made home heaven, in heaven's behoof
I went forth every day, and all day long
Worked for the world. Look, how the laborer's song
Cheers him! Thus sang my soul, at each sharp throe
Of laboring flesh and blood—"She loves me so!"

One day, perhaps such song so knit the nerve
That work grew play and vanished. "I deserve
Haply my heaven an hour before the time!"
I laughed, as silverly the clockhouse-chime
Surprised me passing through the postern-gate
—Not the main entry where the menials wait
And wonder why the world's affairs allow
The master sudden leisure. That was how
I took the private garden-way for once.

Forth from the alcove, I saw start, ensconce
Himself behind the porphyry vase, a man.

My fancies in the natural order ran:
"A spy,—perhaps a foe in ambuscade,—
A thief,—more like, a sweetheart of some maid
Who pitched on the alcove for tryst perhaps."

"Stand there!" I bid.

Whereat my man but wraps
His face the closelier with uplifted arm
Whereon the cloak lies, strikes in blind alarm
This and that pedestal as,—stretch and stoop,—
Now in, now out of sight, he thrids the group
Of statues, marble god and goddess ranged
Each side the pathway, till the gate's exchanged
For safety: one step thence, the street, you know!

Thus far I followed with my gaze. Then, slow,
Near on admiringly, I breathed again,
And—back to that last fancy of the train—
"A danger risked for hope of just a word
With—which of all my nest may be the bird
This poacher covets for her plumage, pray?
Carmen? Juana? Carmen seems too gay
For such adventure, while Juana's grave
—Would scorn the folly. I applaud the knave!
He had the eye, could single from my brood
His proper fledgeling!"

As I turned, there stood
In face of me, my wife stone-still stone-white.
Whether one bound had brought her,—at first sight
Of what she judged the encounter, sure to be
Next moment, of the venturous man and me,—
Brought her to clutch and keep me from my prey:
Whether impelled because her death no day
Could come so absolutely opportune
As now at joy's height, like a year in June
Stayed at the fall of its first ripened rose;
Or whether hungry for my hate—who knows?—
Eager to end an irksome lie, and taste
Our tingling true relation, hate embraced
By hate one naked moment:—anyhow
There stone-still stone-white stood my wife, but now
The woman who made heaven within my house.
Ay, she who faced me was my very spouse
As well as love—you are to recollect!

"Stay!" she said. "Keep at least one soul unspecked
With crime, that 's spotless hitherto—your own!
Kill me who court the blessing, who alone
Was, am, and shall be guilty, first to last!
The man lay helpless in the toils I cast
About him, helpless as the statue there
Against that strangling bell-flower's bondage: tear

Away and tread to dust the parasite,
But do the passive marble no despite!
I love him as I hate you. Kill me! Strike
At one blow both infinitudes alike
Out of existence—hate and love! Whence love?
That 's safe inside my heart, nor will remove
For any searching of your steel, I think.
Whence hate? The secret lay on lip, at brink
Of speech, in one fierce tremble to escape,
At every form wherein your love took shape,
At each new provocation of your kiss.
Kill me!"

We went in.

Next day after this,
I felt as if the speech might come. I spoke—
Easily, after all.

"The lifted cloak
Was screen sufficient: I concern myself
Hardly with laying hands on who for pelf—
Whate'er the ignoble kind—may prowl and brave
Cuffing and kicking proper to a knave
Detected by my household's vigilance.
Enough of such! As for my love-romance—
I, like our good Hidalgo, rub my eyes
And wake and wonder how the film could rise
Which changed for me a barbers' basin straight
Into—Mambrino's helm? I hesitate
Nowise to say—God's sacramental cup!
Why should I blame the brass which, burnished up,
Will blaze, to all but me, as good as gold?
To me—a warning I was overbold
In judging metals. The Hidalgo waked
Only to die, if I remember,—staked
His life upon the basin's worth, and lost:
While I confess torpidity at most
In here and there a limb; but, lame and halt,
Still should I work on, still repair my fault
Ere I took rest in death,—no fear at all!
Now, work—no word before the curtain fall!"

The "curtain"? That of death on life, I meant:
My "word," permissible in death's event,
Would be—truth, soul to soul; for, otherwise,
Day by day, three years long, there had to rise
And, night by night, to fall upon our stage—

Ours, doomed to public play by heritage—
Another curtain, when the world, perforce
Our critical assembly, in due course
Came and went, witnessing, gave praise or blame
To art-mimetic. It had spoiled the game
If, suffered to set foot behind our scene,
The world had witnessed how stage-king and queen,
Gallant and lady, but a minute since
Enarming each the other, would evince
No sign of recognition as they took
His way and her way to whatever nook
Waited them in the darkness either side
Of that bright stage where lately groom and bride
Had fired the audience to a frenzy-fit
Of sympathetic rapture—every whit
Earned as the curtain fell on her and me,
—Actors. Three whole years, nothing was to see
But calm and concord: where a speech was due
There came the speech; when the smiles were wanted too,
Smiles were as ready. In a place like mine,
Where foreign and domestic cares combine,
There 's audience every day and all day long;
But finally the last of the whole throng
Who linger lets one see his back. For her—
Why, liberty and liking: I aver,
Liking and liberty! For me—I breathed,
Let my face rest from every wrinkle wreathed
Smile-like about the mouth, unlearned my task
Of personation till next day bade mask,
And quietly betook me from that world
To the real world, not pageant: there unfurled
In work, its wings, my soul, the fretted power.
Three years I worked, each minute of each hour
Not claimed by acting:—work I may dispense
With talk about, since work in evidence,
Perhaps in history; who knows or cares?

After three years, this way, all unawares,
Our acting ended. She and I, at close
Of a loud night-feast, led, between two rows
Of bending male and female loyalty,
Our lord the king down staircase, while, held high
At arm's length did the twisted tapers' flare
Herald his passage from our palace, where
Such visiting left glory evermore.
Again the ascent in public, till at door
As we two stood by the saloon—now blank
And disencumbered of its guests—there sank

A whisper in my ear, so low and yet
So unmistakable!

"I half forget
The chamber you repair to, and I want
Occasion for one short word—if you grant
That grace—within a certain room you called
Our 'Study,' for you wrote there while I scrawled
Some paper full of faces for my sport.
That room I can remember. Just one short
Word with you there, for the remembrance' sake!"

"Follow me thither!" I replied.

We break
The gloom a little, as with guiding lamp
I lead the way, leave warmth and cheer, by damp
Blind disused serpentining ways afar
From where the habitable chambers are,—
Ascend, descend stairs tunnelled through the stone,—
Always in silence,—till I reach the lone
Chamber sepulchred for my very own
Out of the palace-quarry. When a boy,
Here was my fortress, stronghold from annoy,
Proof-positive of ownership; in youth
I garnered up my gleanings here—uncouth
But precious relics of vain hopes, vain fears;
Finally, this became in after-years
My closet of entrenchment to withstand
Invasion of the foe on every hand—The
multifarious herd in bower and hall,
State-room,—rooms whatsoe'er the style, which call
On masters to be mindful that, before
Men, they must look like men and something more.
Here,—when our lord the king's bestowment ceased
To deck me on the day that, golden-fleeced,
I touched ambition's height,—'t was here, released
From glory (always symbolled by a chain!)
No sooner was I privileged to gain
My secret domicile than glad I flung
That last toy on the table—gazed where hung
On hook my father's gift, the arquebus—
And asked myself, "Shall I envisage thus
The new prize and the old prize, when I reach
Another year's experience?—own that each
Equalled advantage—sportsman's—statesman's tool?
That brought me down an eagle, this—a fool!"

Into which room on entry, I set down
The lamp, and turning saw whose rustled gown
Had told me my wife followed, pace for pace.
Each of us looked the other in the face.
She spoke. "Since I could die now "...

(To explain
Why that first struck me, know—not once again
Since the adventure at the porphyry's edge
Three years before, which sundered like a wedge
Her soul from mine,—though daily, smile to smile,
We stood before the public,—all the while
Not once had I distinguished, in that face
I paid observance to, the faintest trace
Of feature more than requisite for eyes
To do their duty by and recognize:
So did I force mine to obey my will
And pry no further. There exists such skill,—
Those know who need it. What physician shrinks
From needful contact with a corpse? He drinks
No plague so long as thirst for knowledge—not
An idler impulse—prompts inquiry. What,
And will you disbelieve in power to bid
Our spirit back to bounds, as though we chid
A child from scrutiny that's just and right
In manhood? Sense, not soul, accomplished sight,
Reported daily she it was—not how
Nor why a change had come to cheek and brow.)

"Since I could die now of the truth concealed,
Yet dare not, must not die,—so seems revealed
The Virgin's mind to me,—for death means peace
Wherein no lawful part have I, whose lease
Of life and punishment the truth avowed
May haply lengthen,—let me push the shroud
Away, that steals to muffle ere is just
My penance-fire in snow! I dare—I must
Live, by avowal of the truth—this truth—
I loved you! Thanks for the fresh serpent's tooth
That, by a prompt new pang more exquisite
Than all preceding torture, proves me right!
I loved you yet I lost you! May I go
Burn to the ashes, now my shame you know?"

I think there never was such—how express?—
Horror coquetting with voluptuousness,
As in those arms of Eastern workmanship—
Yataghan, kandjar, things that rend and rip,

Gash rough, slash smooth, help hate so many ways,
Yet ever keep a beauty that betrays
Love still at work with the artificer
Throughout his quaint devising. Why prefer,
Except for love's sake, that a blade should writhe
And bicker like a flame?—now play the scythe
As if some broad neck tempted,—now contract
And needle off into a fineness lacked
For just that puncture which the heart demands?
Then, such adornment! Wherefore need our hands
Enclose not ivory alone, nor gold
Roughened for use, but jewels? Nay, behold!
Fancy my favorite—which I seem to grasp
While I describe the luxury. No asp
Is diapered more delicate round throat
Than this below the handle! These denote
—These mazy lines meandering, to end
Only in flesh they open—what intend
They else but water-purlings—pale contrast
With the life-crimson where they blend at last?
And mark the handle's dim pellucid green,
Carved, the hard jadestone, as you pinch a bean,
Into a sort of parrot-bird! He pecks
A grape-bunch; his two eyes are ruby-specks
Pure from the mine: seen this way,—glassy blank,
But turn them,—lo, the inmost fire, that shrank
From sparkling, sends a red dart right to aim!
Why did I choose such toys? Perhaps the game
Of peaceful men is warlike, just as men
War-wearied get amusement from that pen
And paper we grow sick of—statesfolk tired
Of merely (when such measures are required)
Dealing out doom to people by three words,
A signature and seal: we play with swords
Suggestive of quick process. That is how
I came to like the toys described you now,
Store of which glittered on the walls and strewed
The table, even, while my wife pursued
Her purpose to its ending. "Now you know
This shame, my three years' torture, let me go,
Burn to the very ashes! You—I lost,
Yet you—I loved!"

The thing I pity most
In men is—action prompted by surprise
Of anger: men? nay, bulls—whose onset lies
At instance of the firework and the goad!
Once the foe prostrate,—trampling once bestowed,—

Prompt follows placability, regret,
Atonement. Trust me, blood-warmth never yet
Betokened strong will! As no leap of pulse
Pricked me, that first time, so did none convulse
My veins at this occasion for resolve.
Had that devolved which did not then devolve
Upon me, I had done—what now to do
Was quietly apparent.

"Tell me who
The man was, crouching by the porphyry vase!"
"No, never! All was folly in his case,
All guilt in mine. I tempted, he complied."

"And yet you loved me?"

"Loved you. Double-dyed
In folly and in guilt, I thought you gave
Your heart and soul away from me to slave
At statecraft. Since my right in you seemed lost,
I stung myself to teach you, to your cost,
What you rejected could be prized beyond
Life, heaven, by the first fool I threw a fond
Look on, a fatal word to."

"And you still
Love me? Do I conjecture well or ill?"

"Conjecture—well or ill! I had three years
To spend in learning you."

"We both are peers
In knowledge, therefore: since three years are spent
Ere thus much of yourself I learn—who went
Back to the house, that day, and brought my mind
To bear upon your action, uncombined
Motive from motive, till the dross, deprived
Of every purer particle, survived
At last in native simple hideousness,
Utter contemptibility, nor less
Nor more. Contemptibility—exempt
How could I, from its proper due—contempt?
I have too much despised you to divert
My life from its set course by help or hurt
Of your all-despicable life—perturb
The calm I work in, by—men's mouths to curb,
Which at such news were clamorous enough—
Men's eyes to shut before my broidered stuff

With the huge hole there, my emblazoned wall
Blank where a scutcheon hung,—by, worse than all,
Each day's procession, my paraded life
Robbed and impoverished through the wanting wife
—Now that my life (which means—my work) was grown
Riches indeed! Once, just this worth alone
Seemed work to have, that profit gained thereby
Of good and praise would—how rewardingly!—
Fall at your feet,—a crown I hoped to cast
Before your love, my love should crown at last.
No love remaining to cast crown before,
My love stopped work now: but contempt the more
Impelled me task as ever head and hand,
Because the very fiends weave ropes of sand
Rather than taste pure hell in idleness.
Therefore I kept my memory down by stress
Of daily work I had no mind to stay
For the world's wonder at the wife away.
Oh, it was easy all of it, believe,
For I despised you! But your words retrieve
Importantly the past. No hate assumed
The mask of love at any time! There gloomed
A moment when love took hate's semblance, urged
By causes you declare; but love's self purged
Away a fancied wrong I did both loves
—Yours and my own: by no hate's help, it proves,
Purgation was attempted. Then, you rise
High by how many a grade! I did despise—
I do but hate you. Let hate's punishment
Replace contempt's! First step to which ascent—
Write down your own words I re-utter you!
'I loved my husband and I hated—who
He was, I took up as my first chance, mere
Mud-ball to fling and make love foul with!' Here
Lies paper!"

"Would my blood for ink suffice!"

"It may: this minion from a land of spice,
Silk, feather—every bird of jewelled breast—
This poniard's beauty, ne'er so lightly prest
Above your heart there"...

"Thus?"

"It flows, I see.
Dip there the point and write!"

"Dictate to me!
Nay, I remember."

And she wrote the words,
I read them. Then—"Since love, in you, affords
License for hate, in me, to quench (I say)
Contempt—why, hate itself has passed away
In vengeance—foreign to contempt. Depart
Peacefully to that death which Eastern art
Imbued this weapon with, if tales be true!
Love will succeed to hate. I pardon you—
Dead in our chamber!"

True as truth the tale.
She died ere morning; then, I saw how pale
Her cheek was ere it wore day's paint-disguise,
And what a hollow darkened 'neath her eyes,
Now that I used my own. She sleeps, as erst
Beloved, in this your church: ay, yours!

Immersed
In thought so deeply, Father? Sad, perhaps?
For whose sake, hers or mine or his who wraps
—Still plain I seem to see!—about his head
The idle cloak,—about his heart (instead
Of cuirass) some fond hope he may elude
My vengeance in the cloister's solitude?
Hardly, I think! As little helped his brow
The cloak then, Father—as your grate helps me now!

CENCIAJA

Ogni cencio vuol entrare in bucato.—Italian Proverb.

Mr. Buxton Forman, the editor of Shelley, upon asking Browning the precise value attached to the terminal aja in the title of his poem, received the following answer:—

"19 WARWICK CRESCENT, W., July 27, '76.

"DEAR MR. BUXTON FORMAN: There can be no objection to such a simple statement as you have inserted, if it seems worth inserting. 'Fact,' it is. Next: 'aia' is generally an accumulative yet depreciative termination: 'Cenciaja'—a bundle of rags—a trifle. The proverb means 'every poor creature will be pressing into the company of his betters,' and I used it to deprecate the notion that I intended anything of the kind. Is it any contribution to 'all connected with Shelley,' if I mention that my 'Book' (The Ring and the Book) [rather the 'old square yellow book' from which the details were taken] has a reference to the reason given by Farinacci, the advocate of the Cenci, of his failure in the defence of Beatrice? 'Fuisse

punitam Beatricem (he declares) poenâ ultimi supplicii, non quia ex intervallo occidi mandavit insidiantem suo honori, sed quia ejus exceptionem non probavi tibi. Prout, et idem firmiter sperabatur de sorore Beatrice si propositam excusationem probasset, prout non probavit.' That is, she expected to avow the main outrage, and did not: in conformity with her words, 'That which I ought to confess, that will I confess; that to which I ought to assent, to that I assent; and that which I ought to deny, that will I deny.' Here is another Cenciaja!

"Yours very sincerely, ROBERT BROWNING."

May I print, Shelley, how it came to pass
That when your Beatrice seemed—by lapse
Of many a long month since her sentence fell—
Assured of pardon for the parricide—
By intercession of stanch friends, or, say,
By certain pricks of conscience in the Pope
Conniver at Francesco Cenci's guilt,—
Suddenly all things changed and Clement grew
"Stern," as you state, "nor to be moved nor bent,
But said these three words coldly 'She must die;'
Subjoining 'Pardon? Paolo Santa Croce
Murdered his mother also yestereve.
And he is fled: she shall not flee at least!'"
—So, to the letter, sentence was fulfilled?
Shelley, may I condense verbosity
That lies before me, into some few words
Of English, and illustrate your superb
Achievement by a rescued anecdote,
No great things, only new and true beside?
As if some mere familiar of a house
Should venture to accost the group at gaze
Before its Titian, famed the wide world through,
And supplement such pictured masterpiece
By whisper, "Searching in the archives here,
I found the reason of the Lady's fate,
And how by accident it came to pass
She wears the halo and displays the palm:
Who, haply, else had never suffered—no,
Nor graced our gallery, by consequence."
Who loved the work would like the little news:
Who lauds your poem lends an ear to me
Relating how the penalty was paid
By one Marchese dell' Oriolo, called
Onofrio Santa Croce otherwise,
For his complicity in matricide
With Paolo his own brother,—he whose crime
And flight induced "those three words—She must die."
Thus I unroll you then the manuscript.

"God's justice"—(of the multiplicity
Of such communications extant still,
Recording, each, injustice done by God
In person of his Vicar-upon-earth,
Scarce one but leads off to the selfsame tune)—
"God's justice, tardy though it prove perchance,
Rests never on the track until it reach
Delinquency. In proof I cite the ease
Of Paolo Santa Croce."

Many times
The youngster,—having been importunate
That Marchesine Costanza, who remained
His widowed mother, should supplant the heir
Her elder son, and substitute himself
In sole possession of her faculty,—
And meeting just as often with rebuff,—
Blinded by so exorbitant a lust
Of gold, the youngster straightway tasked his wits,
Casting about to kill the lady—thus.

He first, to cover his iniquity,
Writes to Onofrio Santa Croce, then
Authoritative lord, acquainting him
Their mother was contamination—wrought
Like hell-fire in the beauty of their House
By dissoluteness and abandonment
Of soul and body to impure delight.

Moreover, since she suffered from disease,
Those symptoms which her death made manifest
Hydroptic, he affirmed were fruits of sin
About to bring confusion and disgrace
Upon the ancient lineage and high fame
O' the family, when published. Duty bound,
He asked his brother—what a son should do?

Which when Marchese dell' Oriolo heard
By letter, being absent at his land
Oriolo, he made answer, this, no more:
"It must behoove a son,—things haply so,—
To act as honor prompts a cavalier
And son, perform his duty to all three,
Mother and brothers"—here advice broke off.

By which advice informed and fortified
As he professed himself—since bound by birth
To hear God's voice in primogeniture—

Paolo, who kept his mother company
In her domain Subiaco, straightway dared
His whole enormity of enterprise,
And, falling on her, stabbed the lady dead;
Whose death demonstrated her innocence,
And happened,—by the way,—since Jesus Christ
Died to save man, just sixteen hundred years.
Costanza was of aspect beautiful
Exceedingly, and seemed, although in age
Sixty about, to far surpass her peers
The coëtaneous dames, in youth and grace.

Done the misdeed, its author takes to flight,
Foiling thereby the justice of the world:
Not God's however,—God, be sure, knows well
The way to clutch a culprit. Witness here!
The present sinner, when he least expects,
Snug-cornered somewhere i' the Basilicate,
Stumbles upon his death by violence.
A man of blood assaults a man of blood
And slays him somehow. This was afterward:
Enough, he promptly met with his deserts,
And, ending thus, permits we end with him,
And push forthwith to this important point—
His matricide fell out, of all the days,
Precisely when the law-procedure closed
Respecting Count Francesco Cenci's death
Chargeable on his daughter, sons and wife.
"Thus patricide was matched with matricide,"
A poet not inelegantly rhymed:
Nay, fratricide—those Princes Massimi!—
Which so disturbed the spirit of the Pope
That all the likelihood Rome entertained
Of Beatrice's pardon vanished straight,
And she endured the piteous death.

Now see
The sequel—what effect commandment had
For strict inquiry into this last case,
When Cardinal Aldobrandini (great
His efficacy—nephew to the Pope!)
Was bidden crush—ay, though his very hand
Got soil i' the act—crime spawning everywhere!
Because, when all endeavor had been used
To catch the aforesaid Paolo, all in vain—
"Make perquisition," quoth our Eminence,
"Throughout his now deserted domicile!
Ransack the palace, roof and floor, to find

If haply any scrap of writing, hid
In nook or corner, may convict—who knows?—
Brother Onofrio of intelligence
With brother Paolo, as in brotherhood
Is but too likely: crime spawns everywhere."

And, every cranny searched accordingly,
There comes to light—O lynx-eyed Cardinal!—
Onofrio's unconsidered writing-scrap,
The letter in reply to Paolo's prayer,
The word of counsel that—things proving so,
Paolo should act the proper knightly part,
And do as was incumbent on a son,
A brother—and a man of birth, be sure!

Whereat immediately the officers
Proceeded to arrest Onofrio—found
At football, child's play, unaware of harm,
Safe with his friends, the Orsini, at their seat
Monte Giordano; as he left the house
He came upon the watch in wait for him
Set by the Barigel,—was caught and caged.

News of which capture being, that same hour,
Conveyed to Rome, forthwith our Eminence
Commands Taverna, Governor and Judge,
To have the process in especial care,
Be, first to last, not only president
In person, but inquisitor as well,
Nor trust the by-work to a substitute:
Bids him not, squeamish, keep the bench, but scrub
The floor of Justice, so to speak,—go try
His best in prison with the criminal:
Promising, as reward for by-work done
Fairly on all-fours, that, success obtained
And crime avowed, or such connivency
With crime as should procure a decent death—
Himself will humbly beg—which means, procure—
The Hat and Purple from his relative
The Pope, and so repay a diligence
Which, meritorious in the Cenci-case,
Mounts plainly here to Purple and the Hat.

Whereupon did my lord the Governor
So masterfully exercise the task
Enjoined him, that he, day by day, and week
By week, and month by month, from first to last
Toiled for the prize: now, punctual at his place,

Played Judge, and now, assiduous at his post,
Inquisitor—pressed cushion and scoured plank.
Early and late. Noon's fervor and night's chill,
Naught moved whom morn would, purpling, make amends!
So that observers laughed as, many a day,
He left home, in July when day is flame,
Posted to Tordinona-prison, plunged
Into a vault where daylong night is ice,
There passed his eight hours on a stretch, content,
Examining Onofrio: all the stress
Of all examination steadily
Converging into one pin-point,—he pushed
Tentative now of head and now of heart.
As when the nut-hatch taps and tries the nut
This side and that side till the kernel sound,—
So did he press the sole and single point
—What was the very meaning of the phrase
"Do as beseems an honored cavalier"?

Which one persistent question-torture,—plied
Day by day, week by week, and month by month,
Morn, noon and night,—fatigued away a mind
Grown imbecile by darkness, solitude,
And one vivacious memory gnawing there
As when a corpse is coffined with a snake:
—Fatigued Onofrio into what might seem
Admission that perchance his judgment groped
So blindly, feeling for an issue—aught
With semblance of an issue from the toils
Cast of a sudden round feet late so free,
He possibly might have envisaged, scarce
Recoiled from—even were the issue death
—Even her death whose life was death and worse!
Always provided that the charge of crime,
Each jot and tittle of the charge were true.
In such a sense, belike, he might advise
His brother to expurgate crime with ... well,
With Wood, if blood must follow on "the course
Taken as might beseem a cavalier."

Whereupon process ended, and report
Was made without a minute of delay
To Clement, who, because of those two crimes
O' the Massimi and Cenci flagrant late,
Must needs impatiently desire result.

Result obtained, he bade the Governor
Summon the Congregation and despatch.

Summons made, sentence passed accordingly
—Death by beheading. When his death-decree
Was intimated to Onofrio, all
Man could do—that did he to save himself.
'Twas much, the having gained for his defence
The Advocate o' the Poor, with natural help
Of many noble friendly persons fain
To disengage a man of family,
So young too, from his grim entanglement:
But Cardinal Aldobrandini ruled
There must be no diversion of the law.
Justice is justice, and the magistrate
Bears not the sword in vain. Who sins must die.

So, the Marchese had his head cut off,
With Rome to see, a concourse infinite,
In Place Saint Angelo beside the Bridge:
Where, demonstrating magnanimity
Adequate to his birth and breed,—poor boy!—
He made the people the accustomed speech,
Exhorted them to, true faith, honest works,
And special good behavior as regards
A parent of no matter what the sex,
Bidding each son take warning from himself.
Truly, it was considered in the boy
Stark staring lunacy, no less, to snap
So plain a bait, be hooked and hauled ashore
By such an angler as the Cardinal!
Why make confession of his privity
To Paolo's enterprise? Mere sealing lips—
Or, better, saying "When I counselled him
'To do as might beseem a cavalier,'
What could I mean but 'Hide our parent's shame
As Christian ought, by aid of Holy Church!
Bury it in a convent—ay, beneath
Enough dotation to prevent its ghost
From troubling earth!'" Mere saying thus,—'t is plain,
Hot only were his life the recompense.
But he had manifestly proved himself
True Christian, and in lieu of punishment
Got praise of all men!—so the populace.

Anyhow, when the Pope made promise good
(That of Aldobrandini, near and dear)
And gave Taverna, who had toiled so much,
A Cardinal's equipment, some such word
As this from mouth to ear went saucily:
"Taverna's cap is dyed in what he drew

From Santa Croce's veins!" So joked the world.

I add: Onofrio left one child behind,
A daughter named Valeria, dowered with grace
Abundantly of soul and body, doomed
To life the shorter for her father's fate.
By death of her, the Marquisate returned
To that Orsini House from whence it came:
Oriolo having passed as donative
To Santa Croce from their ancestors.

And no word more? By all means! Would you know
The authoritative answer, when folk urged
"What made Aldobrandini, hound-like stanch,
Hunt out of life a harmless simpleton?"
The answer was—"Hatred implacable,
By reason they were rivals in their love."
The Cardinal's desire was to a dame
Whose favor was Onofrio's. Pricked with pride,
The simpleton must ostentatiously
Display a ring, the Cardinal's love-gift,
Given to Onofrio as the lady's gage;
Which ring on finger, as he put forth hand
To draw a tapestry, the Cardinal
Saw and knew, gift and owner, old and young;
Whereon a fury entered him—the fire
He quenched with what could quench fire only—blood.
Nay, more: "there want not who affirm to boot,
The unwise boy, a certain festal eve,
Feigned ignorance of who the wight might be
That pressed too closely on him with a crowd.
He struck the Cardinal a blow: and then,
To put a face upon the incident,
Dared next day, smug as ever, go pay court
I' the Cardinal's antechamber. Mark and mend,
Ye youth, by this example how may greed
Vainglorious operate in worldly souls!"

So ends the chronicler, beginning with
"God's justice, tardy though it prove perchance,
Rests never till it reach delinquency."
Ay, or how otherwise had come to pass
That Victor rules, this present year, in Rome?

FILIPPO BALDINUCCI ON THE PRIVILEGE OF BURIAL

A REMINISCENCE OF A. D. 1676

"No, boy, we must not"—so began
My Uncle (he's with God long since),
A-petting me, the good old man!
"We must not"—and he seemed to wince,
And lost that laugh whereto had grown
His chuckle at my piece of news,
How cleverly I aimed my stone—
"I fear we must not pelt the Jews!

"When I was young indeed,—ah, faith
Was young and strong in Florence too!
We Christians never dreamed of scathe
Because we cursed or kicked the crew.
But now—well, well! The olive-crops
Weighed double then, and Arno's pranks
Would always spare religious shops
Whenever he o'erflowed his banks!

"I 'll tell you"—and his eye regained
Its twinkle—"tell you something choice
Something may help you keep unstained
Your honest zeal to stop the voice
Of unbelief with stone-throw—spite
Of laws, which modern fools enact,
That we must suffer Jews in sight
Go wholly unmolested! Fact!

"There was, then, in my youth, and yet
Is, by our San Frediano, just
Below the Blessed Olivet,
A wayside ground wherein they thrust
Their dead,—these Jews,—the more our shame!
Except that, so they will but die,
Christians perchance incur no blame
In giving hogs a hoist to sty.

"There, anyhow, Jews stow away
Their dead; and—such their insolence—
Slink at odd times to sing and pray
As Christians do—all make-pretence!—
Which wickedness they perpetrate
Because they think no Christians see.
They reckoned here, at any rate,
Without their host: ha, ha! he, he!

"For, what should join their plot of ground

But a good Farmer's Christian field?
The Jews had hedged their corner round
With bramble-bush to keep concealed
Their doings: for the public road
Ran betwixt this their ground and that
The Farmer's, where he ploughed and sowed,
Grew corn for barn and grapes for vat.

"So, properly to guard his store
And gall the unbelievers too,
He builds a shrine and, what is more,
Procures a painter whom I knew,
One Buti (he 's with God), to paint
A holy picture there—no less
Than Virgin Mary free from taint
Borne to the sky by angels: yes!

"Which shrine he fixed,—who says him nay?—
A-facing with its picture-side
Not, as you 'd think, the public way,
But just where sought these hounds to hide
Their carrion from that very truth
Of Mary's triumph: not a hound
Could act his mummeries uncouth
But Mary shamed the pack all round!

"Now, if it was amusing, judge!
—To see the company arrive,
Each Jew intent to end his trudge
And take his pleasure (though alive)
With all his Jewish kith and kin
Below ground, have his venom out,
Sharpen his wits for next day's sin,
Curse Christians, and so home, no doubt!

"Whereas, each phiz upturned beholds
Mary, I warrant, soaring brave!
And in a trice, beneath the folds
Of filthy garb which gowns each knave,
Down drops it—there to hide grimace,
Contortion of the mouth and nose
At finding Mary in the place
They 'd keep for Pilate, I suppose!

"At last, they will not brook—not they!—
Longer such outrage on their tribe:
So, in some hole and corner, lay
Their heads together—how to bribe

The meritorious Farmer's self
To straight undo his work, restore
Their chance to meet and muse on pelf—
Pretending sorrow, as before!

"Forthwith, a posse, if you please,
Of Rabbi This and Rabbi That
Almost go down upon their knees
To get him lay the picture flat.
The spokesman, eighty years of age,
Gray as a badger, with a goat's
Not only beard but bleat, 'gins wage
War with our Mary. Thus he dotes:—

"'Friends, grant a grace! How Hebrews toil
Through life in Florence—why relate
To those who lay the burden, spoil
Our paths of peace? We bear our fate.
But when with life the long toil ends,
Why must you—the expression craves
Pardon, but truth compels me, friends!—
Why must you plague us in our graves?

"'Thoughtlessly plague, I would believe!
For how can you—the lords of ease
By nurture, birthright—e'en conceive
Our luxury to lie with trees
And turf,—the cricket and the bird
Left for our last companionship:
No harsh deed, no unkindly word,
No frowning brow nor scornful lip!

"'Death's luxury, we now rehearse
While, living, through your streets we fare
And take your hatred: nothing worse
Have we, once dead and safe, to bear!
So we refresh our souls, fulfil
Our works, our daily tasks; and thus
Gather you grain—earth's harvest—still
The wheat for you, the straw for us.

"'What flouting in a face, what harm,
In just a lady borne from bier
By boys' heads, wings for leg and arm?'
You question. Friends, the harm is here—
That just when our last sigh is heaved,
And we would fain thank God and you
For labor done and peace achieved,

Back comes the Past in full review!

"'At sight of just that simple flag,
Starts the foe-feeling serpent-like
From slumber. Leave it lulled, nor drag—
Though fangless—forth what needs must strike
When stricken sore, though stroke be vain
Against the mailed oppressor! Give
Play to our fancy that we gain
Life's rights when once we cease to live!

"'Thus much to courtesy, to kind,
To conscience! Now to Florence folk!
There 's core beneath this apple-rind,
Beneath this white-of-egg there 's yolk!
Beneath this prayer to courtesy,
Kind, conscience—there 's a sum to pouch!
How many ducats down will buy
Our shame's removal, sirs? Avouch!

"'Removal, not destruction, sirs!
Just turn your picture! Let it front
The public path! Or memory errs,
Or that same public path is wont
To witness many a chance befall
Of lust, theft, bloodshed—sins enough,
Wherein our Hebrew part is small.
Convert yourselves!'—he cut up rough.

"Look you, how soon a service paid
Religion yields the servant fruit!
A prompt reply our Farmer made
So following: 'Sirs, to grant your suit
Involves much danger! How? Transpose
Our Lady? Stop the chastisement,
All for your good, herself bestows?
What wonder if I grudge consent?

"'—Yet grant it: since, what cash I take
Is so much saved from wicked use.
We know you! And, for Mary's sake,
A hundred ducats shall induce
Concession to your prayer. One day
Suffices: Master Buti's brush
Turns Mary round the other way,
And deluges your side with slush.

"'Down with the ducats therefore!' Dump,

Dump, dump it falls, each counted piece,
Hard gold. Then out of door they stump,
These dogs, each brisk as with new lease
Of life, I warrant,—glad he 'll die
Henceforward just as he may choose,
Be buried and in clover lie!
Well said Esaias—'stiff-necked Jews!'

"Off posts without a minute's loss
Our Farmer, once the cash in poke,
And summons Buti—ere its gloss
Have time to fade from off the joke—
To chop and change his work, undo
The done side, make the side, now blank,
Recipient of our Lady—who,
Displaced thus, had these dogs to thank!

"Now, boy, you 're hardly to instruct
In technicalities of Art!
My nephew's childhood sure has sucked
Along with mother's-milk some part
Of painter's-practice—learned, at least,
How expeditiously is plied
A work in fresco—never ceased
When once begun—a day, each side.

"So, Buti—(he 's with God)—begins:
First covers up the shrine all round
With hoarding; then, as like as twins,
Paints, t' other side the burial-ground,
New Mary, every point the same;
Next, sluices over, as agreed,
The old; and last—but, spoil the game
By telling you? Not I, indeed!

"Well, ere the week was half at end,
Out came the object of this zeal,
This fine alacrity to spend
Hard money for mere dead men's weal!
How think you? That old spokesman Jew
Was High Priest, and he had a wife
As old, and she was dying too,
And wished to end in peace her life!

"And he must humor dying whims,
And soothe her with the idle hope
They 'd say their prayers and sing their hymns
As if her husband were the Pope!

And she did die—believing just
—This privilege was purchased! Dead
In comfort through her foolish trust!
'Stiff-necked ones,' well Esaias said!

"So, Sabbath morning, out of gate
And on to way, what sees our arch
Good Farmer? Why, they hoist their freight—
The corpse—on shoulder, and so, march!
'Now for it, Buti!' In the nick
Of time 't is pully-hauly, hence
With hoarding! O'er the wayside quick
There 's Mary plain in evidence!

"And here 's the convoy halting: right!
Oh, they are bent on howling psalms
And growling prayers, when opposite!
And yet they glance, for all their qualms,
Approve that promptitude of his,
The Farmer's—duly at his post
To take due thanks from every phiz,
Sour smirk—nay, surly smile almost!

"Then earthward drops each brow again;
The solemn task 's resumed; they reach
Their holy field—the unholy train:
Enter its precinct, all and each,
Wrapt somehow in their godless rites;
Till, rites at end, up-waking, lo,
They lift their faces! What delights
The mourners as they turn to go?

"Ha, ha! he, he! On just the side
They drew their purse-strings to make quit
Of Mary,—Christ the Crucified
Fronted them now—these biters bit!
Never was such a hiss and snort,
Such screwing nose and shooting lip!
Their purchase—honey in report—
Proved gall and verjuice at first sip!

"Out they break, on they bustle, where,
A-top of wall, the Farmer waits
With Buti: never fun so rare!
The Farmer has the best: he rates
The rascal, as the old High Priest
Takes on himself to sermonize—
Nay, sneer, 'We Jews supposed, at least,

Theft was a crime in Christian eyes!'

"'Theft?' cries the Farmer. 'Eat your words!
Show me what constitutes a breach
Of faith in aught was said or heard!
I promised you in plainest speech
I 'd take the thing you count disgrace
And put it here—and here 't is put!
Did you suppose I 'd leave the place
Blank therefore, just your rage to glut?

"'I guess you dared not stipulate
For such a damned impertinence!
So, quick, my graybeard, out of gate
And in at Ghetto! Haste you hence!
As long as I have house and land,
To spite you irreligious chaps,
Here shall the Crucifixion stand—
Unless you down with cash, perhaps!'

"So snickered he and Buti both.
The Jews said nothing, interchanged
A glance or two, renewed their oath
To keep ears stopped and hearts estranged
From grace, for all our Church can do;
Then off they scuttle: sullen jog
Homewards, against our Church to brew
Fresh mischief in their synagogue.

"But next day—see what happened, boy!
See why I bid you have a care
How you pelt Jews! The knaves employ
Such methods of revenge, forbear
No outrage on our faith, when free
To wreak their malice! Here they took
So base a method—plague o' me
If I record it in my Book!

"For, next day, while the Farmer sat
Laughing with Buti, in his shop,
At their successful joke,—rat-tat,—
Door opens, and they 're like to drop
Down to the floor as in there stalks
A six-feet-high herculean-built
Young he-Jew with a beard that balks
Description. 'Help ere blood be spilt!'

—"Screamed Buti: for he recognized

Whom but the son, no less no more,
Of that High Priest his work surprised
So pleasantly the day before!
Son of the mother, then, whereof
The bier he lent a shoulder to,
And made the moans about, dared scoff
At sober Christian grief—the Jew!

"'Sirs, I salute you! Never rise!
No apprehension!' (Buti, white
And trembling like a tub of size,
Had tried to smuggle out of sight
The picture's self—the thing in oils,
You know, from which a fresco 's dashed
Which courage speeds while caution spoils)
'Stay and be praised, sir, unabashed!

"'Praised,—ay, and paid too: for I come
To buy that very work of yours.
My poor abode, which boasts—well, some
Few specimens of Art, secures,
Haply, a masterpiece indeed
If I should find my humble means
Suffice the outlay. So, proceed!
Propose—ere prudence intervenes!'

"On Buti, cowering like a child,
These words descended from aloft,
In tone so ominously mild,
With smile terrifically soft
To that degree—could Buti dare
(Poor fellow) use his brains, think twice?
He asked, thus taken unaware,
No more than just the proper price!

"'Done!' cries the monster. 'I disburse
Forthwith your moderate demand.
Count on my custom—if no worse
Your future work be, understand,
Than this I carry off! No aid!
My arm, sir, lacks nor bone nor thews:
The burden 's easy, and we 're made,
Easy or hard, to bear—we Jews!'

"Crossing himself at such escape,
Buti by turns the money eyes
And, timidly, the stalwart shape
Now moving doorwards; but, more wise,

The Farmer—who, though dumb, this while
Had watched advantage—straight conceived
A reason for that tone and smile
So mild and soft! The Jew—believed!

"Mary in triumph borne to deck
A Hebrew household! Pictured where
No one was used to bend the neck
In praise or bow the knee in prayer!
Borne to that domicile by whom?
The son of the High Priest! Through what?
An insult done his mother's tomb!
Saul changed to Paul—the case came pat!

"'Stay, dog-Jew ... gentle sir, that is!
Resolve me! Can it be, she crowned,—
Mary, by miracle,—oh bliss!—
My present to your burial-ground?
Certain, a ray of light has burst
Your vale of darkness! Had you else,
Only for Mary's sake, unpursed
So much hard money? Tell—oh, tell's!'

"Round—like a serpent that we took
For worm and trod on—turns his bulk
About the Jew. First dreadful look
Sends Buti in a trice to skulk
Out of sight somewhere, safe—alack!
But our good Farmer faith made bold:
And firm (with Florence at his back)
He stood, while gruff the gutturals rolled—

"'Ay, sir, a miracle was worked,
By quite another power, I trow.
Than ever yet in canvas lurked,
Or you would scarcely face me now!
A certain impulse did suggest
A certain grasp with this right-hand,
Which probably had put to rest
Our quarrel,—thus your throat once spanned!

"'But I remembered me, subdued
That impulse, and you face me still!
And soon a philosophic mood
Succeeding (hear it, if you will!)
Has altogether changed my views
Concerning Art. Blind prejudice!
Well may you Christians tax us Jews

With scrupulosity too nice!

"'For, don't I see,—let 's issue join!—
Whenever I 'm allowed pollute
(I—and my little bag of coin)
Some Christian palace of repute,—
Don't I see stuck up everywhere
Abundant proof that cultured taste
Has Beauty for its only care,
And upon Truth no thought to waste?

"''Jew, since it must be, take in pledge
Of payment'—so a Cardinal
Has sighed to me as if a wedge
Entered his heart—'this best of all
My treasures!' Leda, Ganymede
Or Antiope: swan, eagle, ape,
(Or what 's the beast of what 's the breed,)
And Jupiter in every shape!

"'Whereat if I presume to ask
'But, Eminence, though Titian's whisk
Of brush have well performed its task,
How comes it these false godships frisk
In presence of—what yonder frame
Pretends to image? Surely, odd
It seems, you let confront The Name
Each beast the heathen called his god!'

"'Benignant smiles me pity straight
The Cardinal.' 'Tis Truth, we prize!
Art 's the sole question in debate!
These subjects are so many lies.
We treat them with a proper scorn
When we turn lies—called gods forsooth—
To lies' fit use, now Christ is born.
Drawing and coloring are Truth.

"''Think you I honor lies so much
As scruple to parade the charms
Of Leda—Titian, every touch—
Because the thing within her arms
Means Jupiter who had the praise
And prayer of a benighted world?
He would have mine too, if, in days
Of light, I kept the canvas furled!'

"'So ending, with some easy gibe.

What power has logic! I, at once,
Acknowledged error in our tribe
So squeamish that, when friends ensconce
A pretty picture in its niche
To do us honor, deck our graves,
We fret and fume and have an itch
To strangle folk—ungrateful knaves!

"'No, sir! Be sure that—what 's its style,
Your picture?—shall possess ungrudged
A place among my rank and file
Of Ledas and what not—be judged
Just as a picture! and (because
I fear me much I scarce have bought
A Titian) Master Buti's flaws
Found there, will have the laugh flaws ought!'

"So, with a scowl, it darkens door—
This bulk—no longer! Buti makes
Prompt glad re-entry; there 's a score
Of oaths, as the good Farmer wakes
From what must needs have been a trance,
Or he had struck (he swears) to ground
The bold bad mouth that dared advance
Such doctrine the reverse of sound!

"Was magic here? Most like! For, since,
Somehow our city's faith grows still
More and more lukewarm, and our Prince
Or loses heart or wants the will
To check increase of cold. 'T is 'Live
And let live! Languidly repress
The Dissident! In short,—contrive
Christians must bear with Jews: no less!'

"The end seems, any Israelite
Wants any picture,—pishes, poohs,
Purchases, hangs it full in sight
In any chamber he may choose!
In Christ's crown, one more thorn we rue!
In Mary's bosom, one more sword!
No, boy, you must not pelt a Jew!
O Lord, how long? How long, O Lord?"

EPILOGUE

μεστοι ...
οἱ δ' ἀμφορῆς οἴνου μέλανος ἀνθοσμίου

"The poets pour us wine—"
Said the dearest poet I ever knew,
Dearest and greatest and best to me.
You clamor athirst for poetry—
We pour. "But when shall a vintage be"—
You cry—"strong grape, squeezed gold from screw.
Yet sweet juice, flavored flowery-fine?
That were indeed the wine!"

One pours your cup—stark strength,
Meat for a man; and you eye the pulp
Strained, turbid still, from the viscous blood
Of the snaky bough: and you grumble "Good!
For it swells resolve, breeds hardihood;
Dispatch it, then, in a single gulp!"
So, down, with a wry face, goes at length
The liquor: stuff for strength.

One pours your cup—sheer sweet,
The fragrant fumes of a year condensed:
Suspicion of all that 's ripe or rathe,
From the bud on branch to the grass in swathe.
"We suck mere milk of the seasons," saith
A curl of each nostril—"dew, dispensed
Nowise for nerving man to feat:
Boys sip such honeyed sweet!"

And thus who wants wine strong,
Waves each sweet smell of the year away;
Who likes to swoon as the sweets suffuse
His train with a mixture of beams and dews
Turned syrupy drink—rough strength eschews:
"What though in our veins your wine-stock stay?
The lack of the bloom does our palate wrong.
Give us wine sweet, not strong!"

Yet wine is—some affirm—
Prime wine is found in the world somewhere,
Of portable strength with sweet to match.
You double your heart its dose, yet catch—
As the draught descends—a violet-smatch,
Softness—however it came there,
Through drops expressed by the fire and worm:
Strong sweet wine—some affirm.

Body and bouquet both?
'T is easy to ticket a bottle so;
But what was the case in the cask, my friends?
Cask? Nay, the vat—where the maker mends
His strong with his sweet (you suppose) and blends
His rough with his smooth, till none can know
How it comes you may tipple, nothing loth,
Body and bouquet both.

"You" being just—the world.
No poets—who turn, themselves, the winch
Of the press; no critics—I 'll even say,
(Being flustered and easy of faith, to-day,)
Who for love of the work have learned the way
Till themselves produce home-made, at a pinch:
No! You are the world, and wine ne'er purled
Except to please the world!

"For, oh the common heart!
And, ah the irremissible sin
Of poets who please themselves, not us!
Strong wine yet sweet wine pouring thus,
How please still—Pindar and Æschylus!—
Drink—dipt into by the bearded chin
Alike and the bloomy lip—no part
Denied the common heart!

"And might we get such grace,
And did you moderns but stock our vault
With the true half-brandy half-attar-gul,
How would seniors indulge at a hearty pull
While juniors tossed off their thimbleful!
Our Shakespeare and Milton escaped your fault,
So, they reign supreme o'er the weaker race
That wants the ancient grace!"

If I paid myself with words
(As the French say well) I were dupe indeed!
I were found in belief that you quaffed and bowsed
At your Shakespeare the whole day long, caroused
In your Milton pottle-deep nor drowsed
A moment of night—toped on, took heed
Of nothing like modern cream-and-curds.
Pay me with deeds, not words!

For—see your cellarage!
There are forty barrels with Shakespeare's brand.
Some five or six are abroach: the rest

Stand spigoted, fauceted. Try and test
What yourselves call best of the very best!
How comes it that still untouched they stand?
Why don't you try tap, advance a stage
With the rest in cellerage?

For—see your cellarage!
There are four big butts of Milton's brew.
How comes it you make old drips and drops
Do duty, and there devotion stops?
Leave such an abyss of malt and hops
Embellied in butts which bungs still glue?
You hate your bard! A fig for your rage!
Free him from cellarage!

'T is said I brew stiff drink,
But the deuce a flavor of grape is there.
Hardly a May-go-down, 't is just
A sort of a gruff Go-down-it-must—
No Merry-go-down, no gracious gust
Commingles the racy with Springtide's rare!
"What wonder," say you, "that we cough, and blink
At Autumn's heady drink?"

Is it a fancy, friends?
Mighty and mellow are never mixed,
Though mighty and mellow be born at once.
Sweet for the future,—strong for the nonce!
Stuff you should stow away, ensconce
In the deep and dark, to be found fast-fixed
At the century's close: such time strength spends
A-sweetening for my friends!

And then—why, what you quaff
With a smack of lip and a cluck of tongue,
Is leakage and leavings—just what haps
From the tun some learned taster taps
With a promise "Prepare your watery chaps!
Here 's properest wine for old and young!
Dispute its perfection—you make us laugh!
Have faith, give thanks, but—quaff!"

Leakage, I say, or—worse—
Leavings suffice pot-valiant souls.
Somebody, brimful, long ago,
Frothed flagon he drained to the dregs; and, lo,
Down whisker and beard what an overflow!
Lick spilth that has trickled from classic jowls,

Sup the single scene, sip the only verse—
Old wine, not new and worse!

I grant you: worse by much!
Renounce that new where you never gained
One glow at heart, one gleam at head,
And stick to the warrant of age instead!
No dwarfs-lap! Fatten, by giants fed!
You fatten, with oceans of drink undrained?
You feed—who would choke did a cobweb smutch
The Age you love so much?

A mine's beneath a moor:
Acres of moor roof fathoms of mine
Which diamonds dot where you please to dig;
Yet who plies spade for the bright and big?
Your product is—truffles, you hunt with a pig!
Since bright-and-big, when a man would dine,
Suits badly: and therefore the Koh-i-noor
May sleep in mine 'neath moor!

Wine, pulse in might from me!
It may never emerge in must from vat,
Never fill cask nor furnish can,
Never end sweet, which strong began—
God's gift to gladden the heart of man;
But spirit 's at proof, I promise that!
No sparing of juice spoils what should be
Fit brewage—mine for me.

Man's thoughts and loves and hates!
Earth is my vineyard, these grew there:
From grape of the ground, I made or marred
My vintage; easy the task or hard,
Who set it—his praise be my reward!
Earth's yield! Who yearn for the Dark Blue Sea's,
Let them "lay, pray, bray"—the addle-pates!
Mine be Man's thoughts, loves, hates!

But some one says, "Good Sir!"
('T is a worthy versed in what concerns
The making such labor turn out well,)
"You don't suppose that the nosegay-smell
Needs always come from the grape? Each bell
At your foot, each bud that your culture spurns,
The very cowslip would act like myrrh
On the stiffest brew—good Sir!

"Cowslips, abundant birth
O'er meadow and hillside, vineyard too,
—Like a schoolboy's scrawlings in and out
Distasteful lesson-book—all about
Greece and Rome, victory and rout—
Love-verses instead of such vain ado!
So, fancies frolic it o'er the earth
Where thoughts have rightlier birth.

"Nay, thoughtlings they themselves:
Loves, hates—in little and less and least!
Thoughts? 'What is a man beside a mount!'
Loves? 'Absent—poor lovers the minutes count!'
Hates? 'Fie—Pope's letters to Martha Blount!'
These furnish a wine for a children's-feast:
Insipid to man, they suit the elves
Like thoughts, loves, hates themselves."

And, friends, beyond dispute
I too have the cowslips dewy and dear.
Punctual as Springtide forth peep they:
I leave them to make my meadow gay.
But I ought to pluck and impound them, eh?
Not let them alone, but deftly shear
And shred and reduce to—what may suit
Children, beyond dispute?

And, here 's May-month, all bloom,
All bounty: what if I sacrifice?
If I out with shears and shear, nor stop
Shearing till prostrate, lo, the crop?
And will you prefer it to ginger-pop
When I 've made you wine of the memories
Which leave as bare as a churchyard tomb
My meadow, late all bloom?

Nay, what ingratitude
Should I hesitate to amuse the wits
That have pulled so long at my flask, nor grudged
The headache that paid their pains, nor budged
From bunghole before they sighed and judged
"Too rough for our taste, to-day, befits
The racy and right when the years conclude!"
Out on ingratitude!

Grateful or ingrate—none,
No cowslip of all my fairy crew
Shall help to concoct what makes you wink,

And goes to your head till you think you think!
I like them alive: the printer's ink
Would sensibly tell on the perfume too.
I may use up my nettles, ere I 've done;
But of cowslips—friends get none!

Don't nettles make a broth
Wholesome for blood grown lazy and thick?
Maws out of sorts make mouths out of taste.
My Thirty-four Port—no need to waste
On a tongue that 's fur and a palate—paste!
A magnum for friends who are sound! the sick—
I 'll posset and cosset them, nothing loth,
Henceforward with nettle-broth!

Robert Browning – A Short Biography

He is the equal of any Victorian Poet that could be mentioned. However, Browning continues to be in the shadow of Tennyson, Arnold, Hopkins, Morris and many others.

Robert Browning was born on May 7th, 1812 in Walworth in the parish of Camberwell, London. He was baptized on June 14th, 1812, at Lock's Fields Independent Chapel, York Street, Walworth.

Browning's early years were certainly very interesting. His mother was an excellent pianist and a very devout evangelical Christian. His father, who worked as a clerk at the Bank of England, was also an artist, scholar, antiquarian, and collector of books and pictures. Indeed, he amassed more than 6,000 volumes of rare books including works in Greek, Hebrew, Latin, French, Italian, and Spanish. For the young and curious Browning, it was a wonderful resource, added to which his father was a guiding force in his education.

Many accounts attest that Browning was already proficient at reading and writing by the age of five. He is said to have been a bright but anxious student and to have studied and learnt Latin, Greek, and French by the time he was fourteen. From fourteen to sixteen he was educated at home, tutored in music, drawing, dancing, and horsemanship. Certainly, language and the arts were two areas the young Browning both absorbed and pushed himself towards.

At the age of twelve he wrote a volume of Byronic verse he called Incondita, which his parents attempted to have published. The attempts were unsuccessful and, disappointed, Browning destroyed the work.

In 1825, a cousin gave Browning a collection of Percy Bysshe Shelley's poetry; Browning was so enamored with the poems that he asked for the rest of Shelley's works for his thirteenth birthday. In fact, Browning then went the extra mile, declaring himself to be both a vegetarian and an atheist in honour of his hero.

Intriguingly it seems that the rejection of his first volume didn't dim his appreciation of other poets, but it appears to have stopped him writing any poems between the ages of thirteen and twenty.

In 1828, Browning enrolled at the newly-opened University of London. He was uncomfortable with the experience and he soon left, anxious to read and absorb at his own pace.

His education which, overall is notably rambling and lacks a structure that many of his artistic contemporaries enjoyed, i.e. excellent public schooling and then a degree at Oxford or Cambridge, may present many of his critics with ammunition to criticize, but alternatively his hap-hazard education certainly contributed to many of the references that baffled both critics and his audience, but they tellingly show the breath and scale of what he could turn words too. What others would call obscure references were, to Browning, remarkably obvious.

Browning's early career was very promising. His long poem Pauline (of which only a fragment was ever finished and published) brought him to the attention of the Pre-Raphaelite master Dante Gabriel Rossetti and his difficult Paracelsus (published in 1835) was warmly admired by both Dickens and Wordsworth.

In the 1830s he met the actor William Macready and was encouraged to develop and turn his talents to the stage by writing verse drama. But these plays, including Strafford, which ran for five nights in 1837, and those contained within the Bells and Pomegranates series, were, for the most part, unsuccessful.

During this period Browning began to discover that his real talents lay in taking a single character and allowing that character to discover more about himself by revealing further personal aspects of himself in his speeches; the dramatic monologue. The techniques he developed through this—especially the use of diction, rhythm, and symbol—are regarded as his most important contribution to poetry. They would later influence such major poets of the 20th Century as Ezra Pound, T. S. Eliot, and Robert Frost.

By 1840, with the publication of Sordello, the tide turned somewhat. Many thought he was being deliberately obscure, opaque beyond measure and his poetry for the next decade or so was not eagerly acquired or talked about.

As Browning attempted to rehabilitate his career he began a relationship with Elizabeth Barrett in 1845. He had read her poems and, being totally charmed by their quality, was determined to meet her. The poetess was better known than the younger Browning but suffered from a debilitating illness and was also subject to the harsh behaviour of her over-bearing father. Nevertheless, the new couple were soon inseparable.

Her father, as he did with any of his children that married, disinherited her. Despite this she had some money from her own resources and sensing that the best outcome for both the relationship and her own health was to move abroad the couple did just that. After a private marriage at St Marylebone Parish Church, in September 1846, they journeyed to Europe to honeymoon in Paris.

Their new life now took them to Italy, first to Pisa and a little later to Florence. There they absorbed life and one another.

But in the short term the literary assault on Browning's work did not let up. He was now criticized by such patrician writers as Charles Kingsley for his abandonment of England for foreign lands. Browning could do little to answer these attacks except to compose with his pen and continue with his poetical journey.

The Browning's were well respected, and even famous. Elizabeth health began to improve, she grew stronger and in 1849, at the age of 43, between four miscarriages, she gave birth to a son, Robert Wiedeman Barrett Browning, whom they nicknamed "Penini" or "Pen",

Intriguingly despite his growing reputation and return to form as a poet he was more often than not known as 'Elizabeth Barrett's husband'.

Work flowed from his pen that was to ensure his reputation as one of England's leading poets. When his collection Men and Women was published in 1855 it contained some of his finest lines. It was dedicated to Elizabeth. Life had begun to smile handsome rewards upon the Brownings.

Victorian society was very much taken with all things spiritualist. It was not enough to have command of much of the globe through Empire, they wished to know and explore wherever they could. The spirit world beckoned their interest. Browning dissented from this view believing it was all a hoax and a fraud. Elizabeth, however, was inclined to believe and this caused several disagreements between the couple.

They attended a séance by Daniel Dunglas Home, in July 1855. (Home was a famous and clamored after Scottish physical medium with the reported ability to levitate and speak with the dead). It is said that during this séance a spirit face materialised. Home then claimed it was the face of Browning's son who had died in infancy. Browning seized the 'materialisation' which turned out to be Home's bare foot. Browning had never lost a son in infancy.

After the séance, Browning wrote an angry letter to The Times, in which he said: "the whole display of hands, spirit utterances etc., was a cheat and imposture."

The Browning's time in Italy were immensely rewarding years for both their personal and professional lives. Browning encouraged her to include Sonnets from the Portuguese in her published works, these beautiful poems are undoubtedly one of the highlights of English love poetry.

Elizabeth had become quite politicised during these years. Engrossed in Italian politics (which was continuing to slowly re-unify the country), she issued a small volume of political poems entitled Poems before Congress (1860) most of which were written to express her sympathy with the Italian cause after the earlier outbreak of The Second Italian Independence War in 1859. In England they caused uproar. Conservative magazines such as Blackwood's and the Saturday Review labelled her a fanatic. She dedicated the book to her husband.

But in 1861 tragedy struck.

The couple had spent the winter of 1860–61 in Rome when Elizabeth's health deteriorated again and they returned to Florence in early June. However, these turned out to be her final weeks. Only morphine would now still the pain. She died in Browning's arms on June 29th, 1861. Browning said that she died "smilingly, happily, and with a face like a girl's .... Her last word was .... "Beautiful".

Her burial took place in the nearby Protestant English Cemetery of Florence. The local people were deeply saddened, and shops closed their doors in grief and respect.

Browning and their son were obviously devastated. Unable to bear being in Florence without Elizabeth they soon returned to London to live at 19 Warwick Crescent, Maida Vale.

As he re-integrated himself back into the London literary scene he began to finally receive the proper praise, respect and reputation that his works deserved.

Browning went on to publish Dramatis Personæ (1864), and The Ring and the Book (1868–1869). The latter, based on an "old yellow book" which told of a seventeenth-century Italian murder trial, received wide and generous critical acclaim. Although by now he was in the twilight of a long and prolific career, that had achieved some notable ups and downs, he was respected and indeed renowned for his talents and works.

In 1878, he revisited Italy for the first time since Elizabeth's death. He would return there on several further occasions but never to Florence.

Such was the esteem he was held in that The Browning Society was founded in 1881. Although he had never obtained a degree (something that set him apart from many other Victorian poets) he was now awarded honorary degrees from Oxford University in 1882 and then the University of Edinburgh in 1884.

In 1887, Browning produced the major work of his later years, Parleyings with Certain People of Importance in Their Day. Browning now spoke with his own voice as he engaged in a series of dialogues with long-forgotten figures of literary, artistic, and philosophic history. Unfortunately, both the critics and public were completely baffled by this.

On April 7th, 1889 Browning attended a dinner party at the home of his friend, the artist Rudolf Lehmann. The highlight of which was a recording made on a wax cylinder on an Edison cylinder phonograph. On the recording, which still exists, Browning recites part of How They Brought the Good News from Ghent to Aix, and can even be heard apologising when he forgets the words.

The recording was first played in 1890 on the anniversary of his death, at a gathering of his admirers, it was said to be the first time anyone's voice 'had been heard from beyond the grave'.

His last work Asolando: Fancies and Facts (1889), returned to his brief and concise lyric verse that was so popular. It was published on the day of his death on December 12th, 1889, Robert Browning was at his son's home Ca' Rezzonico in Venice.

He was buried in Poets' Corner in Westminster Abbey; his grave lies immediately adjacent to that of Alfred Tennyson.

Among the many who have publicly acknowledged their literary debt to him are Henry James, Oscar Wilde, George Bernard Shaw, G. K. Chesterton, Ezra Pound, Jorge Luis Borges, and Vladimir Nabokov.

Here follows a list of the plays and poetry volumes published during his lifetime. Poems of particular worth are noted from within those volumes.

Pauline: A Fragment of a Confession (1833)
Paracelsus (1835)
Strafford (play) (1837)
Sordello (1840)
Bells and Pomegranates No. I: Pippa Passes (play) (1841)
    The Year's at the Spring
Bells and Pomegranates No. II: King Victor and King Charles (play) (1842)
Bells and Pomegranates No. III: Dramatic Lyrics (1842)
    Porphyria's Lover
    Soliloquy of the Spanish Cloister
    My Last Duchess
    The Pied Piper of Hamelin
    Count Gismond
    Johannes Agricola in Meditation
Bells and Pomegranates No. IV: The Return of the Druses (play) (1843)
Bells and Pomegranates No. V: A Blot in the 'Scutcheon (play) (1843)
Bells and Pomegranates No. VI: Colombe's Birthday (play) (1844)
Bells and Pomegranates No. VII: Dramatic Romances and Lyrics (1845)
    The Laboratory
    How They Brought the Good News from Ghent to Aix
    The Bishop Orders His Tomb at Saint Praxed's Church
    The Lost Leader
    Home Thoughts from Abroad
    Meeting at Night
Bells and Pomegranates No. VIII: Luria and A Soul's Tragedy (plays) (1846)
Christmas-Eve and Easter-Day (1850)
An Essay on Percy Bysshe Shelley (essay) (1852)
Two Poems (1854)
Men and Women (1855)
    Love Among the Ruins
    A Toccata of Galuppi's
    Childe Roland to the Dark Tower Came
    Fra Lippo Lippi
    Andrea Del Sarto
    The Patriot
    The Last Ride Together
    Memorabilia
    Cleon
    How It Strikes a Contemporary
    The Statue and the Bust
    A Grammarian's Funeral
    An Epistle Containing the Strange Medical Experience of Karshish, the Arab Physician
    Bishop Blougram's Apology
    Master Hugues of Saxe-Gotha
    By the Fire-side

Dramatis Personae (1864)
> *Caliban upon Setebos*
> *Rabbi Ben Ezra*
> *Abt Vogler*
> *Mr. Sludge, "The Medium"*
> *Prospice*
> *A Death in the Desert*

The Ring and the Book (1868–69)
Balaustion's Adventure (1871)
Prince Hohenstiel-Schwangau, Saviour of Society (1871)
Fifine at the Fair (1872)
Red Cotton Night-Cap Country, or, Turf and Towers (1873)
Aristophanes' Apology (1875)
> *Thamuris Marching*

The Inn Album (1875)
Pacchiarotto, and How He Worked in Distemper (1876)
> *Numpholeptos*

The Agamemnon of Aeschylus (1877)
La Saisiaz and The Two Poets of Croisic (1878)
Dramatic Idylls (1879)
Dramatic Idylls: Second Series (1880)
> *Pan and Luna*

Jocoseria (1883)
Ferishtah's Fancies (1884)
Parleyings with Certain People of Importance in Their Day (1887)
Asolando (1889)
> *Prologue*
> *Summum Bonum*
> *Bad Dreams III*
> *Flute-Music, with an Accompaniment*
> *Epilogue*

www.ingramcontent.com/pod-product-compliance
Lightning Source LLC
Chambersburg PA
CBHW060143050426

42448CB00010B/2270